Gun Policy in the United States and Canada

Gun Policy in the United States and Canada

The Impact of Mass Murders and
Assassinations on Gun Control

Anthony K. Fleming

continuum

Continuum International Publishing Group

The Tower Building   80 Maiden Lane
11 York Road   Suite 704
London SE1 7NX   New York NY 10038

www.continuumbooks.com

ISBN: 978-1-4411-0650-6 (hardcover)

Library of Congress Cataloging-in-Publication Data
Fleming, Anthony K.
  Gun policy in the United States and Canada : the impact of mass murders and assassinations on gun control / Anthony K. Fleming.
    p. cm.
  Includes bibliographical references and index.
  ISBN-13: 978-1-4411-0650-6 (hbk. : alk. paper)
  ISBN-10: 1-4411-0650-2 (hbk. : alk. paper) 1. Gun control–United States. 2. Gun control–Canada. 3. Violent crimes–United States. 4. Violent crimes–Canada. I. Title.

HV7436.F58 2012
363.330973–dc23   2011043970

Typeset by Newgen Imaging Systems Pvt Ltd, Chennai, India
Printed in the United States of America

This book is dedicated to my mother and father.
Without their love and support I wouldn't be
who I am today.

Contents

Preface   viii

1. An Introduction to Political Culture and Gun
    Control Policy in the United States and Canada   1

2. Agenda Setting, Institutions, and Interest Groups
    in the United States and Canada   22

3. The United States: Violence Leads Nowhere   53

4. Canada: Violent Events Drive Change   99

5. Conclusions: A Discussion of Why Canada Reacts to
    Gun Violence Events and the United States Does Not   127

6. Gun Control Policy in the United States and
    Canada: 2008 to Present   135

Bibliography   144

Index   153

Preface

This book discusses the importance of firearms-related focusing events in two states: the United States and Canada. It is my contention that focusing events can lead to items being placed on the agenda; however, interest group activity can either impede or promote the policy outcomes due to the event.

I argue that in the United States firearms-related focusing events often lead to new policy being placed on the agenda when there is a Democratic government; however, due to the diffuse nature of the American political system and the presence of the NRA (a staunchly status quo group) policy rarely, if ever, goes to the formulation stage. Furthermore, when there is a Republican government in power, focusing events lead to fewer policy alternatives being placed on the agenda, much less advancing to the formulation stage.

Alternatively, in Canada, firearms-related focusing events will lead to an item being placed on the agenda when there is a left-of-center government. Due to public outcry (from the masses and more importantly interest groups), and motivated policy entrepreneurs within government; policy makers will react quickly and decisively in creating new firearms legislation. There are two reasons for this: centralized power of the Parliament, and the minimization of status quo interest group influence due to the blocking of alternative venues in the short term after a focusing event. This minimization of influence for these groups means that focusing events not only lead to new firearm legislation being placed on the agenda, but also allows other actors inside of government, in particular left-of-center policy entrepreneurs, to have significant power in policy making in the short term. When there is a right-of-center government, firearms-related focusing events will lead to the policy being placed on the agenda, but rather than having major overhauls to the subsystem, changes will be incremental in nature, if they occur at all.

Chapter 1

An Introduction to Political Culture and Gun Control Policy in the United States and Canada

Introduction

In 2007 at Virginia Tech, a lone gun man executed arguably the worst mass murder in modern US history. Yet, even after such a tragedy, new restrictive federal gun control policy was not created. In 1989, a similar event took place in Canada; a lone gun man perpetrated what is known as the Montreal Massacre. Unlike in the United States, Canada took action in less than two years. New comprehensive gun control policy was created and eventually led to the creation of the Gun Registry.

These two very similar events had drastically different outcomes. In the United States very little happened at the federal level, in Canada there were broad and sweeping changes made to gun control legislation at the federal level. It is my contention that the structure of a states government, along with interest group pressures and political parties, play a significant role in dampening or accelerating the effects of a focusing event. Presidential systems, like in the United States, react slowly to events such as the Virginia Tech slayings. They react slowly, in part, because of the diffuse nature of power in presidential systems. Parliamentary systems, especially effectively unicameral ones, are more centralized in power and this enables them to react quickly to focusing events.

Interest group pressures also have significant impact. Dominant status quo interest groups are capable of preventing the passage of new legislation in a presidential system. Yet, in a parliamentary system, interest groups may not be able to react quickly enough to provide the Parliament with alternative ideas to prevent change, or they may be unable to influence government significantly because of lack of access or party discipline.

If a pro-change interest group is the most powerful interest group in a presidential system, change may come, but it will be slow, and will take multiple events to cause change. In a parliamentary system, if a pro-change interest group is the most powerful, change can occur very rapidly. In order to test the theory I study firearms-related focusing events in the United States and Canada.

The US Presidential Institutional Structure vs Canadian Parliamentary Institutional Structure

It is necessary to discuss the basic differences between presidential and parliamentary systems before going into a more in-depth discussion. Presidential systems are generally diffuse. The executive and the legislature are different and coequal entities. This allows for a natural cooling-off period for the creation of legislation after a focusing event.

Parliamentary systems have concentrated power. The executive and the legislature are, in fact, the same branch of government. This allows for policy to be passed rapidly during periods of high emotion; especially when there is a single party majority. This means that the public and interest groups have very little time to try and dissuade the policy makers from a particular course of action (Lijphart 1999, pp. 10–21).

In presidential systems, the executive is always elected by the public. Parliamentary systems differ because the executive is chosen by the legislature. This leads to a centralization of power in a single branch of government, the executive (Lijphart 1999, pp. 10–21). In Canada, power is centralized in the House of Commons, with the Senate taking a less substantial role in policy making. For the party in power to be able to wield power in a way to ensure its policies are implemented, parties need a working majority of the seats in the lower house, and the party must have strict party cohesion. This is very different from the United States where legislators freelance and are themselves their own "enterprise" (Salisbury and Shepsle 1981).

Of particular importance, parties must be able to have the majority of the seats without forming a coalition. Lijphart argues that when a party does not hold the majority of the seats and must enter into a coalition, this weakens the hold of a government's policy-making abilities. He goes on to suggest that in states where you have multiple powerful parties that are capable of preventing one party from receiving 50% of the legislative vote, you will find that the ability of parties to control policy making at their discretion is significantly reduced. However, when there is a disciplined majority party system in a Parliament, Lijphart finds that the efficiency and the power of the dominant party to act and disregard the minority allows for there to be an "elective dictatorship" (Lijphart 1999, pp. 12–13). The "elective dictatorship" reference suggests that policy making can be quick and efficient in parliamentary states.

In presidential systems the minority groups (primarily interest groups) can still play a role in the creation of policy. There are many access points for the formulation of policy. Minority groups are able to block or limit the scope of many pieces of legislation. In parliamentary systems, there are few access points and only one body that can create legislation, the majority party or coalition in the House of Commons. This means that minority groups have a nearly insurmountable mountain to climb when trying to influence policy making. Lijphart even suggests that minority groups are completely excluded from policy making and their sole role is to be that of the opposition (Lijphart 1999, p. 11). If all minority groups are marginalized (minority parties and opposing interest groups), then the ability of policy to go from the agenda-setting stage to the formulation stage should be relatively unimpeded by these groups when compared to presidential states.

The Key Variables of the Study: A Discussion of the Structure of Government, Parties, and Interest Groups

As mentioned earlier in the chapter, the structure of government is particularly important in determining the outcome of a focusing event. The presidential structure of the United States is diffuse and this allows for there to be multiple locations where interest groups can access the policy process and either promote or dissuade the creation of policy. In Canada, on the other hand, the parliamentary system there allows for an efficient creation of policy because of power being concentrated in one branch of government, in Canada's case, the House of Commons. These structural differences between the two countries, in my theoretical opinion, are a prime factor in determining the outcome of focusing events and whether the influence from them will lead to agenda attention and ultimately policy creation.

The second major variable in this book is the impact of parties. In the United States there are two major political parties, the Republicans and the Democrats. The Republicans, as a general rule, favor lenient gun control legislation and the Democrats favor more restrictive gun control legislation. The influence that the National Rifle Association (NRA) has on both of these parties, in particular, the Republican Party is discussed in future chapters.

In Canada, there are multiple parties. Left-of-center parties heavily support more restrictive gun control. Right-of-center parties usually support lenient legislation. However, the interest group dynamics are different in Canada than in the United States. Arguably the most influential interest group in Canada is the Coalition for Gun Control which is a passionately pro-gun control group.

Thus, when we consider parties in both countries, it is important to understand that right-of-center groups support lenient gun controls and left-of-center groups support restrictive gun controls. Because of the political leanings of parties, it is important to understand their impact on policy creation when they are in control of government after a major focusing event.

Finally, we must consider the importance of interest groups and their role in creating or dissuading policy. In the United States, the most powerful and most important interest group is the NRA. Its influence has been felt throughout the entirety of my study. In Canada, the most influential interest group is the Coalition for Gun Control. Its impact on policy making in Canada began after the 1989 Montreal Massacre, but its influence has grown considerably since.

In the United States the most influential interest groups is the NRA. The NRA is an old organization; it was originally created in 1871. Initially, the NRA was primarily a gun club that helped its members easily obtain surplus military weapons and to train individuals to shoot firearms more accurately. Originally, it was not an organization that was overly concerned with politics, For example, the restrictive federal gun control legislation that was created in 1934 was not significantly attacked by the NRA. However, in the 1960s when the federal government began turning its interests to the topic of gun control after multiple infamous assassinations, the NRA became far more political.

The political role of the NRA has been felt by many Congressional members in Washington. The results of the 1994 election, in which the Republicans took overwhelming control of the House of Representatives, has often been attributed by Democrats, in particular, President Clinton, to the NRA. The influence of the NRA on the 1994 election is explored more thoroughly in Chapter 3.

The NRA's membership has also grown significantly since the 1960s. In the mid-1970s, there were nearly a million NRA members; this number has steadily increased. In 2001, NRA membership had increased to well over 4 million. The NRA also has a significant budget. By 2001, the NRA had a budget of $168 million dollars, and was working with very little debt. It hired 300 employees with 65 specifically devoted to lobbying efforts (Spitzer, pp. 75–6). With its strong membership base, large budget, and its single-minded purpose in defeating gun control legislation the NRA has become the most influential gun policy interest group in the United States.

The NRA's primary opponent is the Brady Campaign, formerly Handgun Control Inc. It was initially created in 1974, by a Republican businessman Pete Shields whose son was murdered by a firearm. Handgun Control Inc. was significantly hindered by lack of resources until the 1980s. After the wounding of Presidential Press Secretary James Brady, his wife, Sarah, joined the executive board of Handgun Control Inc., and eventually took over leadership of the organization. The organization was then renamed the Brady Campaign.

The Brady Campaign has attempted, ironically, to duplicate the tactics of the NRA in order to gain influence. They have worked to build a grassroots base of membership, demonize the opposition, influence its members to contribute money, and for its members to call politicians. However, when compared to the NRA's membership and funding it falls short. For example, the membership of the Brady Campaign in 1998 was 400,000 and its annual budget was only $7 million dollars (Spitzer, pp. 94–5). The discrepancy in membership and funding demonstrates some key reasons why the NRA has been able to continue its stranglehold on gun control policy.

In Canada, unlike the United States, gun control groups have been far more influential in impacting gun control policy. Arguably the most powerful interest group that lobbies gun control in Canada is the Coalition for Gun Control which is headed by Wendy Cukier. The Coalition for Gun Control was created in a direct response to the Montreal Massacre. Its goals are: possession permits for all gun owners, a cost effective way to register all guns, a total ban on assault weapons and large capacity magazines, regulation of ammunition, and stricter handgun control laws (www.guncontrol.ca). Though statistics on its membership and funding have been difficult to find, it is evident through actions of Canadian politicians and from reactions from the media and antigun control groups that this interest group is the primary mover and shaker on restrictive gun control legislation in Canada.

The primary lenient gun control group in Canada is the National Firearms Association (NFA). The NFA was created in 1978 by David Tomlinson. The NFA has similar goals to its counterpart in the United States, but hasn't been as successful in preventing gun control legislation as the NRA. The NFA states that it quests for fair and practical firearm and property legislation within Canada. The NFA goes on to say that it is "Canada's firearms voice in Ottawa" (www.nfa.com). Like the Coalition for Gun Control, statistics on its membership and funding have been difficult to access.

Stages of the Policy Process: A Quick Overview

In this section, the stages of the policy process are described. Throughout the book I mention the impact of focusing events on the policy process; in particular, the impact focusing events have on agenda setting and formulation. Thus, it is important to understand where agenda setting and formulation fall within the policy process.

Thomas Dye defines the six stages of the policy process. The first stage of the policy process is the problem identification stage. At this stage there is the identification of policy problems and there will be demands by some groups for policy action. The second stage is known as agenda setting. At this stage there is a focusing of attention of the mass media and public officials on specific public problems to decide how to handle a policy issue. The third stage is policy formulation. At this stage there is a development of policy proposals by interest groups, Congressional committees, and think tanks. The fourth stage is policy legitimation. At this stage there is a selection and enactment of policies through political actions by Congress, the president, and the court. The fifth stage is policy implementation. At this stage, the policies are implemented by organized bureaucracies, public expenditures, and by the activities of executive agencies. The final stage of the policy process is policy evaluation. At this stage the policies of government are evaluated by bureaucracies, the media, the public, and government itself (Dye, p. 14).

The main stages of the policy process that I am concerned with in this book are: agenda setting, formulation, policy legitimation, and to a lesser extent implementation. The one difference between my descriptions and Dye is that I combine policy formulation and policy legitimation and make it into one stage. The reason I do this is because formulation as defined by Dye is the creation of policy by the combined forces of interest groups and Congressional members; policy legitimation is the step of taking these policies and then enacting them. Thus, I see that there is a very fine line between the two, and when I discuss policy formulation in this book it will mean a combination of both of these stages.

Gun Culture Differences between the United States and Canada: Should Gun Culture be Used as an Explanatory Variable?

There are significant cultural differences between the United States and Canada. These differences are important for us to understand in order to have a more concrete grasp of why gun control focusing events have such a significant variation in response from one country to the next.

Lipset (1990) argues that the United States and its beliefs derive from the American Revolution. The American people revolted against their oppressors in Great Britain in order to form a new independent nation. This uprising has had its lingering effects on American culture. One such effect is that Americans have a natural dislike for authority. Americans tend to see the state and authority in a negative way. This stems from the ideas and ideals that were implanted in the American psyche after the American Revolution.

Another effect that has risen in the United States is the belief in civil liberties and individualism. Americans believe that they should have the right to act independently and not be interfered with by the state. Americans are also more driven to succeed individually and are less concerned about communal success.

This tradition of distrusting government and valuing liberty has its roots in the founding of the United States. The US government is designed in a way to prevent the government from being all powerful and overly intrusive into American lives. The Bill of Rights was also established to ensure liberty and undeniable rights to individuals.

The political culture that was created after the American Revolution led to the United States adopting an inefficient presidential system. It also has led to the powerful interest group structure that we see in the United States. Every American believes in civil liberties, but not all Americans believe in the same civil liberties. This has led to the creation of groups who seek to promote a certain liberty, and others who seek to deny it. We can see that this clearly applies to gun control. The NRA at its most basic form is a group seeking to protect the civil liberty of gun ownership whereas the Brady Campaign seeks to deny this liberty.

Canada is different than the United States. Canadians are the people who did not rebel against the British. The Canadians viewed the rebellious Americans to the south as "rabble-rousers." The Canadians had a peaceful break with the British. Canada did not begin separating from the United Kingdom until 1867. In 1982, Canada asked the United Kingdom to relinquish formal control of authority over the Canadian constitution. The United Kingdom accepted the request. It is interesting to note also that Canada relied heavily on the United Kingdom for a variety of issues. Canadian citizens were not their own separate citizenry until 1947, and the highest court in Canada was the Privy Council of Great Britain until 1982 (Lipset, p. 46).

The most important cultural item that came from the creation of Canada is the deference to the state and to laws. Canadians are far more likely to acquiesce to the state. Canadians are far more community centered. Canadians are also less concerned about liberties and are more concerned with stability and security. Canadians believe that giving away certain liberties in order to maintain social order is common sense. Even with the 1982 passage of the Canadian Charter of Rights, which greatly enhanced individual and group liberties in Canada, Canadians are still more community and society oriented than Americans.

The different political culture that we see in Canada led to the creation of a very different political environment than what we see in the United States. The government in Canada is a parliamentary system which has fewer checks and allows for government to work quickly and efficiently. The public did not distrust government like they did in the United States, thus they did not see the need to create a presidential system, which has numerous checks and balances. The United States created the separation of the main branches of government because they distrusted the power of it. This distrust came from the hatred for the United Kingdom and its taxes during the Revolutionary War.

Interest groups that seek to protect civil liberties are less important in Canada than in the United States. The fundamental right to civil liberties that is felt in the United States is not as important to most Canadians. This has led to interest groups that seek to protect civil liberties in Canada, such as the NFA, to be much weaker than groups that seek to protect public safety rather than civil liberties, such as the Coalition for Gun Control.

The differences in political culture give us some understanding why each country has developed in the way that it has. We have a more solid understanding of why Americans formed a presidential system and the Canadians a parliamentary one. We also understand why interest groups promoting civil liberties in the United States have stronger support than those that seek to deny them; and we also understand why in Canada interest groups promoting public safety and security have stronger support than those who promote civil liberties.

Kopel (1992) explains why there is a difference in views in relation to gun control policy in Canada when compared to the United States. He argues that Canada views its Mounties and the law in a positive light, which helps explain why Canadians are far more likely to accept the gun laws of the government whereas the American hero, the cowboy, is more likely to take matters into his own hands to protect himself from threats whether they be outlaws or a corrupt government. Kopel suggests this fundamental difference between gun cultures is one of the prime reasons that the publics of the United States and Canada have differences in gun control opinions. However, not all agree that the differences in gun control opinion between the publics of the United States and Canada are that different.

Political culture is a powerful underlying reason why different countries organized themselves in different ways. It also helps us understand why certain types of interest groups are more strongly supported in some countries and less supported in others. But does it explain the reaction to focusing events that government institutions and interest groups have?

Mauser and Margolis (1992) argue that the political culture in the United States and Canada don't differ very much when it comes to gun control policy. They find that Canadians generally favor stricter gun control legislation than in the United States; however, the margin is not as significant as often perceived. They find that majorities of the population in both countries favor moderate gun control legislation such as background checks and firearms licensing. The one major discrepancy that they found is that Canadians own fewer handguns and favor much more restrictive controls on them. However, Mauser and Margolis argue that gun control policy differs significantly between the two countries for institutional reasons and not cultural ones.

They argue that the parliamentary nature of the Canadian government allows for Canadians to pass gun control policy without much interference from the general public. They also argue that the nature of Canadian political institutions allows for only certain interest groups to have access and prevents many interest groups from having any say at all. At the time of publication, they found that gun control groups on both sides of the fence were poorly organized and had very little influence in determining the outcome of gun control policy. Another important factor is that members of Parliament are more insulated from public pressures than their counterparts in the United States. In sum, they find that institutional factors in Canada better explain gun control policy differences than cultural explanations.

Like Mauser and Margolis, I argue that culture has an indirect impact on the policy that is created after an event. I argue that the form of governmental institutions plays a more significant role in determining the outcome of a focusing event than political culture. The presidential system in the United States makes it difficult to create policy quickly, even if everyone was desirous of a quick outcome. The parliamentary system in Canada allows for policy to be passed quickly and efficiently. I suggest that historical political culture may have led to why and how these institutions were formed, but political culture does not make them function the way that they do today. Thus, political culture is why government institutions were designed the way that they were at the birth of each nation, but political culture does not necessarily dictate how these institutions will behave. Their behavior is a product of their design.

When considering culture and interest groups, it is understandable as to why the NRA is powerful in the United States and its counterpart in Canada is weak. However, a majority of people in both states, and an overwhelming majority at that, believe in stricter gun control laws (Schuman and Presser 1977; Lindaman and Haider-Markel 2002). The NRA is a minority group supporting a minority opinion in the United States, and the NFA is minority group supporting a minority opinion in Canada. Yet, the NRA is far more influential than the NFA. Why?

Based on the previous arguments by Lipset and Kopel, I could suggest that it is a cultural argument. However, if it were purely cultural why would the opinion of the general masses be trumped in the United States in favor of a minority opinion? I believe that the NRA is far more powerful than its counterpart in Canada, not for cultural reasons, but because of its organization and its access to politicians. This access that the NRA has is due in large part because of the design of American institutions which allow for multiple access points. Thus, I suggest that we consider culture a factor, but that we pay more attention to the importance of the structure of government organization in both states. The importance of interest group system structure and the access points that interest groups have (or do not have) in each of these states are more important factors in determining why each state behaves the way that it does after a gun violence focusing event.

The Gun Control Situation: A Historical Perspective on the United States and Canada

The United States

The United States has had many infamous assassinations and mass murders over the past 60 years. Some of the most noted took place in the 1960s with the assassinations of John F. Kennedy, his brother Robert Kennedy, and Martin Luther King Jr. Due to the multiple assassinations in the 1960s, Congress passed the Gun Control Act of 1968. The bill was first proposed in 1963, but because of the NRA and its allies in Congress it died each year in committee, only to be proposed again the next year until it finally was passed. However, this was the first major piece of legislation to tackle the gun control debate since the 1930s (Spitzer, p. 112). In signing the legislation, President Lyndon Johnson said, "Today we begin to disarm the criminal and the careless and the insane," but he lamented that the bill fell short because "we just could not get Congress to carry out the requests . . . for the national registration of all guns and the licensing of those who carry guns" (http://www.enotes.com/gun-violence).

Support for the passage of the bill increased significantly after the assassination of Robert Kennedy. The bill was voted on and passed in the House of Representatives the day after Robert Kennedy was assassinated and two months after the assassination of Martin Luther King Jr. However, the Gun Control Act of 1968 met vigorous opposition from the NRA and its allies. This influence watered down significant portions of the provisions that were initially sought by gun control advocates, specifically the blanket registration and licensing of all firearms that were proposed by President Johnson (Spitzer, p. 115).

The Gun Control Act of 1968 banned the interstate shipment of firearms and ammunition, prohibited the sales of firearms to minors, drug addicts, mental incompetents and convicted felons, strengthened licensing and record-keeping requirements for gun dealers and collectors, extended federal regulation and taxation to "destructive devices" such as land mines, bombs, hand grenades, and the like; increased penalties for those who used guns in the commission of a crime covered by federal laws, and banned the importation of foreign-made surplus firearms, except those appropriate for sporting purposes (Spitzer, p. 115). Spitzer argues that this was a modest change to gun control legislation because Johnson had been pushing for blanket registration and licensing requirements.

The impact of the legislation was actually minimal because the number of gun dealers and the importations of shotguns increased, as did the domestic ownership of all firearms.

The next major focusing event of note took place 13 years after the passage of the Gun Control Act of 1968. On March 30, 1981, John Hinckley fired six bullets at President Ronald Reagan in the space of three seconds, hitting Reagan, a police officer and a Secret Service agent, and seriously wounding of Reagan Press Secretary James Brady. It took twelve years and two administrations later before President Clinton signed the Brady Bill, which required a waiting period and background check on all handguns purchased through licensed dealers (www.pbs.org). However, immediately following this focusing event, no new federal gun control legislation was created until 1986. Interestingly, the gun control legislation of 1986 made gun control laws in the United States *weaker*. In 1986, the Firearms Owners Protection Act was passed. The bill was proposed by Senator James McClure (Republican of Idaho) and Representative Harold Volkmer (Democrat Missouri). The main goal of this bill was to repeal some provisions of the legislation that had been passed in the Gun Control Act of 1968. The NRA began heavy lobbying efforts in order to obtain enough votes for the bill to become law. Their actions worked. The bill was passed in the Senate with a vote of 79–15 and in the House with a vote of 292–130 (Spitzer, pp. 117–18).

The Firearms Owners Protection Act amended the 1968 legislation. Interstate sales of rifles and shotguns became legal. It eliminated record-keeping requirements for ammunition dealers, made it easier for individuals selling guns to do so without a license unless they did so regularly, allowed gun dealers to do business at gun shows, and prohibited the Bureau of Alcohol, Tobacco, and Firearms (BATF) from issuing regulations requiring centralized records of gun dealers. The act also limited the BATF to one unannounced inspection a year of gun dealers and prohibited the establishment of any form of comprehensive firearms registration (Spitzer, p. 118).

The next major gun event took place on January 17, 1989, in Stockton, California: 25-year-old Patrick Purdy fired an AK-47 at random at Cleveland Elementary School, killing 5 children (aged between 6 and 9) and wounding 29 others and 1 teacher before taking his own life. The incident inspired a rash of legislation restricting the purchase of assault weapons in California and set the scene for more attempts at federal legislation (Davidson 1993).

This event laid the groundwork for the Assault Weapons Ban. The Assault Weapons Ban proposed the banning of weapons with fully automatic fire. There were some definitional problems in what was included as an assault weapon, which made it difficult to pass. President George H. W. Bush initially was against the ban, but after the Stockton shooting he became a supporter of the bill. However, the Assault Weapons Ban languished in committees (Spitzer, p. 121).

In 1991, George J. Hennard killed 22 people and himself in Killeen, Texas. This event was the worst mass murder in the United States until the Virginia Tech shooting of 2007. The Senate included provisions for an assault weapons ban in its crime bill for that year. The House, which voted on the ban the day after the Killeen, Texas Massacre, removed the Assault Weapon Ban from the bill. So, even though there were two mass slayings in a time frame of a little more than two years, no new federal gun control legislation was passed even though it was vigorously debated and was actually passed in the Senate (Spitzer, p. 121).

On November 30, 1993, the Brady Bill was signed into law. The Brady Bill had been hotly contested in the House and Senate for nearly six years. The Bill required a five-business-day waiting period for handgun purchases; it also authorized $200 million dollars a year for states to upgrade their criminal records, increased the price of federal firearms licensing, made it a federal crime to steal from licensed dealers, and made police engage in reasonable efforts to check the background of gun buyers. The last provision, that of police checking the background of gun buyers was later found to be unconstitutional by the Supreme Court in the case of *Printz v. US* (Spitzer, pp. 129–30). The provisions of the Brady Bill were not exceptionally extensive. Once it became law, it was still attacked by lenient gun control proponents and since its inception has had a great deal of its power removed.

In 1994, the Assault Weapons Ban was once again proposed. With the urging of President Clinton, who was an avid supporter of the ban, the Senate passed the bill. The Assault Weapons Ban was once again proposed to the House and this time there was success. The House Judiciary Committee approved the bill, and it was sent to the floor for a final vote. The bill was passed with a vote of 216–214. The Assault Weapons Ban was for all intents and purposes a modest bill. It outlawed for 10 years the sale and possession of 19 specified weapons. The bill also specifically exempted 661 sporting rifles and limited gun clips to those that could only hold 10 bullets or less. Existing assault rifles were exempted from the ban (Spitzer, pp. 122–4). The Assault Weapons Ban was a significant piece of legislation that followed on the heels of the Brady Bill; even so, it was fairly modest in its goals. The ten-year provision of the ban was not renewed. The bill has since expired and assault weapons that were banned are once again legal for purchase.

It is not conclusive which focusing events impacted the creation of the Brady Bill and the Assault Weapons Ban the most; however, what we do find is that gun control legislation in the United States has been modest when compared to Canada. The legislation that has been passed, the Assault Weapons Ban and the Brady Bill, were initially successful, but later either expired in the case of the Assault Weapons Ban or were weakened significantly by the Courts.

Unfortunately, the Killeen, Texas slaying was not the last major firearms focusing event in the United States. Since then there have been several major focusing events, but new federal gun control legislation has not been created. On April 20, 1999, the most infamous high school shooting in the United States took place. The shootings at Columbine High School provided one of the most powerful symbols to be attached to the gun control policy issue. On April 26, 1999, President Clinton appealed to Congress to limit access to explosives and firearms. And on April 27, 1999, the President, the First Lady, and others tried appealing to Congress to have their gun control legislation placed on the agenda.

However, the political battling by the Democrats and Republicans resulted in a standstill. The Democrats tried to push more restrictive firearm control policy through the two chambers. They were met with stiff resistance from Republicans and the NRA. The Democrats attempted to get the support of the public, but this support waned after the legislative process was drawn out over a longer period of time. Because of this, the power of the symbols that attached to the policy in response to the focusing event was allowed to decrease and subsequently no new federal laws were created (Spitzer, pp. 132–3).

Since Columbine, there have been even more school shootings and massacres. In the past few years, two shootings took place at major universities. The Virginia Tech shooting was the worst mass murder in US history. Another mass slaying took place at Northern Illinois University. Even so, at this point in time, very little new legislation has been created at the federal level (during the 110th Congress, 2007 to 2008, a tweak was made to the instant background check to make it easier to use).

In the United States, gun control policy has been passed, but it has been very modest in comparison to other states. In fact, two pieces of legislation that were created during the 109th Congress, 2005 to 2006, once again set the stage for more lenient gun control legislation. The first piece of legislation prevented gun manufacturers from being liable for their products causing death or injury. The second piece of legislation prevented the ability of the federal government from seizing firearms during times of crisis.

The major restrictive federal legislation that has been created has often been dismantled by the NRA and its Republican allies. We also find that focusing events draw attention to the issue, but do not always lead to new policy. Interestingly, as Birkland (2006) argues, a single focusing event may not be enough to drive a policy to the formulation stage, but multiple events in a short period of time may lead to new legislation. All three pieces of restrictive legislation that were discussed took place after multiple focusing events in less than a two-year period. The Gun Control Act of 1968 was passed after both Martin Luther King Jr and Robert Kennedy were assassinated in a period of less than six months. The Assault Weapons Ban and the Brady Bill were both passed after the Purdy Massacre and the Killeen, Texas Massacre, which took place in a period of less than two years. However, more recently we have seen a plethora of focusing events, from the multiple high school shootings that culminated in the worst, Columbine, to the two major university shootings, Virginia Tech and Northern Illinois, and yet we still see very little federal legislation created. I argue that this is due to the power of the NRA, coupled with its relationship with members of government, in particular Republicans and Democrats from rural states. The diffuse nature of American political institutions facilitates the ability of the NRA to attack new gun control legislation at multiple access points within government.

Canada

The first piece of major gun control legislation took place in 1934. This legislation required the registering of handguns with the Royal Canadian Mounted Police. In 1969, after a series of terrorist activities in Quebec, Bill C-150, the Criminal Law Amendment Act, was proposed. It created a list of restricted, nonrestricted and prohibited firearms. For the first time, police had the right to search for firearms and seize them without a warrant from a judge when the police believed that the firearm could be potentially harmful even if the firearm was not being used in the commission of a crime. Bill C-150 also implemented for the first time registration certificates; these certificates had to be obtained for each individual firearm a buyer purchased (www.cfc-ccaf.gc.ca).

In 1976, Bill C-83 was introduced. It proposed stricter penalties for firearms crimes, the prohibition of all automatic weapons, requiring any buyer to obtain a license to purchase a firearm or firearm ammunition, and at the age of 18 anyone using a firearm must also obtain a license. Applicants for licenses would also have to have two written documents from references stating that they were of firm mind and body in order to obtain a license. Bill C-83 did not become law, but many of its provisions were reintroduced the following year (www.cfc-ccaf.gc.ca).

In 1977, Bill C-51, a watered down version of Bill C-83, was passed. It required potential firearms purchasers to seek Firearms Acquisition Certificates. In order to obtain a firearm, a potential purchaser had to have a background check. The law prohibited the ownership of fully automatic weapons, unless they had already been registered or would be registered by January 1, 1978 (www.cfc-ccaf.gc.ca).

The December 6, 1989, Montreal Massacre perpetrated by Marc Lepine was the first of several high-profile shootings that led to drastic changes in the gun legislation in Canada. Lepine targeted and slaughtered 14 women. He forced the men to leave the classroom so that he could shoot the women. In 1990, immediately following the events of the Lepine shooting, Bill C-80 was proposed. Even though Bill C-80 failed to become law, the provisions that were introduced in it would lay the foundation for the proposals in Bill C-17 introduced in 1991 (www.cfc-ccaf.gc.ca).

Both critics and supporters say the Coalition for Gun Control, which was born after the Montreal Massacre, was instrumental in the passage of Bill C-17 in 1991 under a Conservative government (Wilson-Smith 1999). In 1991, the Senate approved the firearms control legislation, Bill C-17. The law made all Firearms Acquisition Certificate (FAC) applicants take a safety course, pass a thorough background check, and wait 28 days after applying to receive a FAC for the purchase of a firearm to obtain another FAC for the purchase of a second firearm; it also placed more restrictions on handguns, ammunition magazines, and semiautomatic rifles (www.cfc-ccaf.gc.ca).

In 1992 there were two other high-profile killings that drew in particular the interest of the Coalition for Gun Control and led them to recommending more restrictive gun control measures. The Coalition called the first event the Yeo Inquest, in which a violent offender out on bail used his legally owned rifle and shot and killed two women. Also in 1992, a disgruntled university professor shot and killed four other academics at Concordia University. The Coalition for Gun Control recommended the registration of all firearms in Canada after the events (www.guncontrol.ca). These events, coupled with the Montreal Massacre, led to even larger changes in gun control policy when the Liberals took back control of Parliament.

In 1993, the Liberals regained control under the direction of Prime Minister Jean Chretien. The Liberals began in earnest to implement a system not to only register all firearms, but also to register their owners. Thus, the stage was set for the Canadian Firearms Registry to be created (Brown-John 2003).

On April 5, 1994, Georgina Leimonis was shot and killed by an immigrant to Canada (McDonald 1995). The result of this shooting was that the parliament met not only to create stricter gun control legislation, Bill C-68, but to create stricter immigration laws. New gun control laws were created in the form of the Firearms Act of 1995. All rifles and shotguns now had to be registered, a new licensing system was to be implemented to replace the FAC system, and the possession of a license was required to buy ammunition. The Canadian Firearms Center was given the task of creating a new licensing system (www.cfc-ccaf.gc.ca).

The Firearms Act was given a phasing in period by the Canadian Parliament. The laws and regulations created by it did not begin until December 1, 1998. As of January 1, 2001, all Canadians had to obtain a license to purchase firearms or ammunition. As of January 1, 2003, all Canadians needed to obtain a valid registration certificate for all firearms in their possession, including nonrestricted rifles and shotguns (www.cfc-ccaf.gc.ca).

The Vernon Massacre in 1996 was another major focusing event in Canada. It resulted in the death of nine people and the suicide of the shooter. On November 27, 1996, Allan Rock, Minister of Justice and Attorney General of Canada, made a statement in the House of Commons regarding the proposed amendments to make the Firearms Act even more restrictive. "The goal of the new regulations is to keep guns out of the hands of criminals and to help keep Canada safe," said Minister Rock. "We have put in place measures to prevent violence, to do everything we can to reduce the number of tragedies such as the Vernon Massacre. Canada is well on its way to implementing one of the toughest and most effective gun control laws in the world" (McDonald 1995).

The Firearms Act did not pass without meeting opposition. Alberta and other western provinces challenged the validity of it almost immediately. However, the Canadian Supreme Court upheld the validity of the law. Even though the Firearms Act was held to be valid, it has had major failings. Various problems have arisen that have made many question its effectiveness, even its former supporters (Brown-John 2003).

The Firearms Act is an example of drastic policy change that was implemented in response to firearms violence. However, with the number of problems that it has had, perhaps the Firearms Act is an example of why politicians like to make incremental changes rather than drastic ones when drafting policy.

The problems that have arisen with the Firearms Act have led to various attempts to modify the system. In 2001, under Liberal government Bill C-15 became law. Its goals were to relax the screening process on firearms and to extend grandfathering for prohibited firearms. The bills goal was also to make it easier for firearms owners to comply with the legislation. When the Conservatives took over control of Parliament in 2006, they attempted to introduce lenient gun control legislation to further modify the Gun Registry and to remove some of its provisions. But these attempts failed.

Canada has only had a few major focusing events; however, gun control policy has been created after these major focusing events. Gun control policy before the Montreal Massacre was moderate. Canada's gun control measures were stiffer than in the United States, but they were not nearly as stringent as they have become. Since the Montreal Massacre, Canada has prided itself on its strict gun control laws.

One major difference between Canada and the United States is the lack of a major pro-firearms group. In the United States the NRA has been capable of limiting gun control legislation, but the same cannot be said for Canada. The NFA is not nearly as powerful as its American counterpart. The lack of a powerful pro-firearms group at the time of these events, coupled with Canada's parliamentary system, may be the primary reason focusing events there have led to significant change.

Comparing the United States with Canada

There is a clear difference between gun control policies in the United States when compared to Canada. The United States has had relatively weak laws created to regulate firearms, and there have been laws passed to protect gun owners. In Canada, gun control laws have become more and more restrictive over time. The United States' drastic difference in gun control laws when compared to Canada is a curious phenomenon. Why is there such a difference between gun control policy responses after a focusing event in the United States and Canada? Is it because of interest groups, governmental institutions, parties, political culture, or a combination of the four?

Pal (2003), argues that the variance in gun control legislation between the United States and Canada is based on two fundamental issues: the structure of government, and the role of institutions. Pal argues that because of the parliamentary system in Canada, it is far easier for gun control legislation to be created there. In the United States, the diffuse nature of institutions and the access of interest groups, in particular the NRA makes it very difficult for new restrictive gun control legislation to be created.

In Canada, gun control legislation falls under criminal law, and criminal law is made almost exclusively at the federal level. This gives the central government extreme power in making gun control legislation. Pal also argues that because parliamentary systems are far more efficient at making policy, this allows for gun control to be created more easily there. Pal also concludes that focusing events lead to gun control legislation in Canada, but not the United States (Pal, p. 254). The reason for this is because of the design of Canadian institutions, which allow for the Canadian government to create policy more quickly and easily than its American counterpart. This institutional arrangement allows the Canadian government to impose losses to interest groups and others in society with more ease than in the United States.

In the United States gun control legislation is rarely considered. Pal argues that the only time gun control legislation is considered is when there is an assassination or massacre, a strong push by the president for there to be new gun control laws, and through executive orders. However, the latter two rarely happen (Pal, p. 244). Gun control legislation is far more likely to fail in the United States than in Canada. The main reasons given for failure are: the NRA blocks or impedes legislation, the structure of the legislature, and the NRA exacts punishments on legislators who do not accept the proposals made by the NRA (Pal, p. 245).

Pal's argument about the importance of institutions and government structure in the creation of gun control policy is very interesting. My theory will be testing the same propositions made by Pal, but will be focusing more on the impact of assassinations and massacres and less on the role of the executive. I believe that the focusing events and the structure of government are the primary factor that leads to change in Canada (with interest groups having less power), and that interest groups, political parties, and institutional structure of the legislature are the primary variables that prevents change in the United States. I believe that the executive is important in the policy process in the United States and Canada, but the executive in most cases is reacting to a focusing event when proposing new legislation and is not actually going to be attempting to create new gun control policy without a galvanizing event.

Design of the Book: A Brief Overview of Future Chapters

Chapter 2 discusses key literature on the United States and Canada. The literature is divided into two sections; each section discusses the key literature on agenda setting, institutions, and interest groups. After covering the literature on each state, the chapter discusses where the literature converges and diverges in regard to agenda setting and it also discusses interest groups and institutions and where the literature converges/diverges. Also of particular interest and importance to my theory is the discussion of focusing events.

In Chapter 2 the literature on agenda setting, focusing events, institutions, and interest groups are merged cross-nationally and across time in order to obtain a better understanding of not only the American policy-making system, but also of Canada. It is my contention throughout this work that gun violence focusing events play a major role in the passage of policy in Canada, but are not nearly as important in the United States due to the built-in checks and balances of presidential systems and the power of a staunchly status quo group, the NRA. This assumption is based on the fact that presidential systems are structured in a way for there to be many access points, which means that there are many places for a piece of legislation to die; this enables status quo interest groups to block the passage of new legislation rather than assisting pro-change interest groups in lobbying for the creation of new policy. I also contend that interest groups in Canada will not be as powerful in preventing the passage of policy after a focusing event because of the centralized control of power in parliamentary systems, especially if the party or parties in power are adversarial to the status quo interest group's goals.

Chapter 3 focuses on the United States. The time period of my study ranges from the Kennedy Assassination in 1963 to 2008. This section assesses a variety of ways in which Americans view the gun control issue. It also demonstrates that gun control policy does not necessarily coincide well with the views of the majority of the public.

Second, I discuss bill proposals in relation to focusing events. I do this by using the *Congressional Index* to sort all bills that were proposed on gun control from 1963 to 2008. The bills were coded as being restrictive, meaning the bill wanted to make the obtaining of firearms and their parts more difficult, or lenient, meaning the bill wanted to make the obtaining of firearms and their parts more lenient. The discussion in this portion of Chapter 3 indicates that gun violence events do impact agenda setting, but not necessarily formulation.

The third section takes an overview of the *New York Times* and its coverage of focusing events, interest groups, and policy outcomes. This portion of Chapter 3 allows for an in-depth understanding of the political environment at the time of the event and which individuals and groups were very important in the creation or the prevention of new gun control policy.

Chapter 4 studies Canadian gun control policy. The time period of my study in Canada is more narrowly focused, 1989 to 2008. The first section of this chapter goes into a discussion of public opinion on various aspects of gun control. This allows for a well-rounded discussion of whether gun control attitudes have varied over time. It also provides a more in-depth overview of the gun culture within Canada, and whether gun control policy attitudes have increased or decreased over time.

The second section of Chapter 4 focuses on bill introduction and formulation in Parliament. This section covers the introduction of government bills into Parliament whose main focus was gun control. Unlike the United States, where there were literally hundreds of gun control bills proposed since 1963, the number of gun bills proposed are far lower. This section examines each gun bill proposed, which party proposed it, and whether it became law or not.

The third section of Chapter 4 uses the *Globe and Mail* to find articles, opinions, and discussions about politicians and interest groups and proposed gun control policy in Canada after major focusing events. This allows for a more in-depth understanding of the attitudes of the public, policy makers, and interest groups at the time of the event. This section goes into a more in-depth discussion of each focusing event at the time of the event and subsequent news coverage.

Chapter 5 compares the similarities between the United States and Canada on the subject of gun control. The first portion compares public opinion in the United States and Canada on the subject of gun control. The second portion compares bill introduction and agenda attention to gun control policy in the United States and Canada. The final portion compares the activity of interest groups in the United States and Canada. The book ends with a discussion of the main theme of the book and that is: Why is the United States less responsive to gun violence focusing events than Canada?

Chapter 2

Agenda Setting, Institutions, and Interest Groups in the United States and Canada

Agenda Setting: United States

When subjects land on the agenda, they seem to hit all of the participants inside government at the same time (Kingdon 1984). This statement is the theoretical basis behind the garbage can model of agenda setting (see also Cohen, March, and Olson 1972). The garbage can model contains problems and solutions of various kinds that are proposed by participants as they are generated (Kingdon 1984). These problems and solutions come from three streams: the problem stream, the solution stream, and the political stream. The three streams intersect to provide for the opening of what Kingdon refers to as policy windows, which are opportunities for drastic policy change. Policy windows enable participants in policy making, particularly policy entrepreneurs, avenues to create policy change.

Kingdon argues that policy entrepreneurs act in three different ways. First, they try to elevate their particular policy concern to the agenda. Second, they try to soften up the policy makers by lobbying them with letters, hearings, and press coverage. Third and most important to this book is that they engage in "coupling" (205). Coupling is when a policy entrepreneur drives home his or her pet project when there is a propitious moment. This propitious moment is when a policy window opens. For there to be new policy created, a policy entrepreneur must be ready and able to drive home their pet project (Kingdon 1984, pp. 204–5). One thing that is evident from Kingdon's discussion of policy entrepreneurs is that policy windows are the ideal time for policy entrepreneurs to act if they want policy change. But what causes policy windows to open?

According to Kingdon, entrepreneurs are capable of driving home policy when a policy window opens. Kingdon focuses heavily on policy change, and not as much on the status quo. Birkland (1997) argues that policy entrepreneurs press for policy change that favor their goals, but status quo policy entrepreneurs will be seeking limited change or none at all after a focusing event (19).

Baumgartner and Jones (1993) argue that policy entrepreneurs attempt to have their alternatives made into policy. They suggest that new ideas are constantly being proposed and can lead to the instability of a policy monopoly, an arrangement where key members of the government work closely with a certain interest group or groups to create policy. I suggest that multiple new ideas could be proposed by policy entrepreneurs in a policy monopoly when there is a focusing event. Thus, because of the proposal of multiple policy alternatives after a focusing event, it leads the policy monopoly to be at its most unstable and allows for the opportunity for policy change.

One of the primary variables that lead to the opening of policy windows is the increase of public attention. Scholars have indicated repeatedly the responsiveness of government officials to public opinion. Congressional members respond to their constituencies because of electoral concerns (Mayhew 1974), and more recent studies have indicated that the government is responsive to public opinion on a macro level (Erikson et al. 2002).

Erikson et al. (1995) find that when the public calls for a more liberal or a more conservative government, politicians oblige. When the public mood is liberal, we tend to see liberal policies made, and when the public mood is conservative we tend to see conservative policies. Large-scale shifts in public opinion lead to large-scale shifts in public policy. The public mood shifts slowly because the public becomes disillusioned with conservative or liberal policies and wants change. The party that is in power passes ideologically driven policies that alienate the general public. Thus, the overall mood of the American public slowly begins to shift from liberal to conservative or conservative to liberal, due to the actions of the party in power. The authors argue that long-term shifts in public opinion will lead to change in policy. So, just how long does public opinion have to be heightened before it leads to new public policy?

Interestingly, Schuman and Presser's (1977) survey research of the general public on attitudes toward police gun registration of all firearms discovered some startling conclusions. They found that an overwhelming percentage of the public have over time favored gun registration, but they also found that those who opposed the gun registration control were far more prepared to become politically active in their opposition than those who favored gun control registration. They argue that because the people who write letters and meet with legislators are most often the intense dissenters, policy makers believe that these dissenters are actually more representative of the public than what they actually are, which is a primary reason that the majority opinion for firearms registration has been widely ignored.

In the same realm of thought, Lindaman and Haider-Markel's (2002) study of party elites, members of the House and Senate, and mass opinion finds that there is a clear divergence between Democratic elites and Republican elites on the gun control issue, and this divergence has grown in recent years. In 1970, 30% of Democrats favored gun control and in 1999, 84% favored stricter gun control legislation. In 1970, 29% of Republicans favored gun control and in 1999, 34% favored stricter gun control legislation; thus there was a 4% difference in elite opinion in 1970 versus a 50% difference in elite opinion in 1999. On the flip side of the issue, a very high percentage of the public has always favored gun control. The Democrats are actually more in line with mass public opinion than the Republicans (p. 101). Yet as demonstrated in the Schuman and Presser article, the minority opinion and the Republican Party have been quite capable at preventing new gun control legislation in the United States.

Counter to the Erikson et al. piece, gun control policy appears to be unique. Long-term support by the majority of the public has led to very little gun control policy. The long-term public opinion has generally favored stricter gun control legislation, but as evidenced by Schuman and Presser (1977) and Lindaman and Haider-Markel (2002), this does not seem to be important enough to lead to the creation of new restrictive gun control policy. So, what could cause change to the gun control policy realm? If not long-term steady pressure, perhaps violent shocks to the system will lead to new gun control policy?

Baumgartner and Jones (1993) advance a theory of punctuated equilibrium. The punctuated equilibrium theory builds upon the work of Kingdon, but instead of focusing predominantly on incremental change, the authors wish to explain periods of sweeping, rapid change. According to the punctuated equilibrium theory, policy windows can open wide enough for volatile change to occur. Rapid, sweeping change is a result of changing policy definitions, the attachment of new symbols, and positive feedback. Most issue change occurs during periods of heightened general attention to the policy. In the process of agenda-setting, the degree of public indifference to a given problem changes dramatically.

Media attention to public policy tends to follow a pattern of either feast or famine. Important political questions are often ignored for years, but during certain periods almost every general media outlet features similar stories prominently. External shocks to the system affect all relevant policy-making institutions simultaneously, causing change in each of them rather than in only one or a few. This can lead to the mobilization of the normally apathetic. Depending on the degree of apathy that prevails, different groups will see their views adopted as the majority view. As the level of apathy changes, so do majority opinions.

Punctuations can be so powerful, in fact that they can make even strict party discipline states react against their own party platform. Walgrave et al. (2008) in their study of parties and a large number of policy agendas in Belgium find that punctuations to the system have a startling impact. Belgium is a parliamentary state that has very cohesive party structure. Belgium's party discipline more closely resembles Canada in that regard than it does with the United States. But Walgrave et al. find that when there are external shocks to the system, the media and the public pressure parties into considering policy to which they may be ideologically opposed. This suggests that punctuations and focusing events may be able to trump party power. However, in the United States, where party cohesion is much less important, gun violence focusing events rarely lead to significant changes to the system, even when there is a strong outcry by the media and the public. This suggests that interest group power is far more relevant in the creation of policy in the United States than in other countries.

Downs (1972) looks at agenda setting and policy change in terms of an issue attention cycle. These stages include (1) a pre-problem stage, (2) a discovery and enthusiasm stage, (3) a realization of cost stage, (4) a gradual decline of interest stage, and finally, (5) a post-problem stage. The argument Downs makes in his model is that major policy changes are unlikely to occur, and indeed many policies never come to fruition, because of the realization of costs involved with making the policy. Essentially, the process is often too slow for there to be policy change. The public is most likely to accept broad and sweeping change immediately after an event. However, due to the diffuse nature of institutions in the United States, it takes too much time for policy to be formulated and implemented. This leads to a decline in enthusiasm and support for new policies leading to no change. However, Downs does not apply his theory to parliamentary systems. In these systems, change can be very rapid due to centralization of power. Downs' theory is more applicable when applied to the United States, because Parliaments are less diffuse in nature and policy can be passed quickly during times of heightened attention and enthusiasm.

In my summary of the key authors, Kingdon (1984) argues that the garbage can model accounts mostly for incremental change, but periods of drastic change can occur. Baumgartner and Jones (1993) use their punctuated equilibrium model to account for non-incremental change. With this in mind, it is reasonable to ask several questions that emerge from the literature. What factors can lead to periods of punctuation or, in the Downs model, what factors could lead to a policy reaching the discovery and enthusiasm stage? Why do items go from the agenda-setting stage to the formulation stage, or why do they go to the agenda-setting stage but never go any further? My argument is that focusing events play a major role in forcing gun control policy alternatives on the public agenda in the United States, but are not successful in forcing gun control policy to be formulated due to the multiple factors in the United States: government institutions, political parties, and the NRA.

Kingdon (1984) describes focusing events as a "crisis or disaster that comes along to call attention to the problem, a powerful symbol that catches on, or the personal experience of a policymaker" (pp. 94–5). In Kingdon's interviews of actors inside government, 35% mentioned focusing events as important factors in agenda setting.

The emergence and diffusion of powerful symbols is another variation of a focusing event. The subject is already on the minds of important people, and a symbol comes along to focus their attention. Symbols act as reinforcements for something already taking place and as something that rather powerfully focuses the attention, rather than as a prime mover in agenda setting. Symbols catch on and have important focusing effects because they capture in a nutshell some sort of reality that people already sense in a vague, more diffuse way (Kingdon 1984, p. 97).

Many authors have argued that focusing events only rarely carry a subject to policy agenda prominence by themselves. They need to be accompanied by something else. First, they can serve to focus attention on a problem. Second, a focusing event can lead to attention to something that could be considered a problem if subsequent consideration really establishes there was a widespread condition that needs attention. Third, focusing events can affect problem definition in combination with other similar events. Awareness of a problem sometimes comes with the second crisis, not the first, because the second cannot be dismissed as an isolated fluke, as the first could (Kingdon 1984, p. 98).

Cobb and Elder (1983) recognized the importance of what they called "circumstantial reactors" in leading to the reconsideration of policies. Sabatier (1991) accounted for focusing events within the advocacy-coalition framework, studying how events influence policy making and politics within policy domains and communities. Baumgartner and Jones (1993) also describe focusing events as one of several factors capable of bringing about rapid change.

Focusing events are successful at bringing about agenda attention because of the powerful policy images they can leave imprinted on the minds of citizens and policy makers. Focusing events, such as disasters or tragedies, offer new opportunities to attach new symbols to policies. This allows the policy definition and image to change, and often leads to periods of opened policy windows or punctuated equilibrium. However, policy change is not guaranteed; there are many factors that can lead to its prevention.

Birkland (1997) studies focusing events such as natural disasters, oil spills, and nuclear power plant accidents where agendas were controlled through the expansion and containment of an issue. A focusing event is defined by Birkland as being:

> an event that is sudden, relatively rare, can be reasonably defined as harmful or revealing the possibility of potentially greater future harms, inflicts harms or suggests potential harms that are or could be concentrated on a definable geographical area or community of interest, and that is known to policy makers and the public virtually simultaneously. (Birkland 1997, p. 21)

Birkland describes four criteria for focusing events. The first criterion is that such events happen suddenly, with little or no warning. Sudden events are associated with "spikes" of intense public interest and agenda activity that are attributable to a particular event. Interest groups that seek to prevent these issues from becoming elevated on the agenda will find it very difficult to keep them off the news agenda and institutional agendas. Conversely, groups that seek to elevate an issue on the agenda can use these events to attract greater attention to the problem revealed by the event or take advantage of the event to attach their pet solution to an existing problem with a new symbol (Birkland 1997, p. 23).

The second criterion is that the event is generally rare. Even if we did know that the event was coming, we may never be able to fix the precise location or time of the next catastrophe. The rarity of an event is closely related to its suddenness; rare events cannot be predicted, and thus strike with little or no warning. The more frightening the event, the more focal attention it will gather (Birkland 1997, p. 23).

The third criterion is that the event affects a large number of people. These people can be from the same geographic area or from the same communities. They also can consist of the public or policy makers, attentive or inattentive to politics. Often, focusing events can lead to the inattentive becoming suddenly attentive to politics because they want action regarding the important issue associated with the event (Birkland 1997, p. 24).

The fourth and final criterion is that the public and most informed members of the policy community learn of a focusing event virtually simultaneously. These events can very rapidly alter mass and elite consciousness of a social problem. Since the event comes to the mass and elite consciousness simultaneously, issue containment or expansion strategies must be employed hurriedly and almost on the fly; neither side of the ensuing debate is able to time the occurrence of events and plan, in any detail, their responses to them. In short, potential focusing events are important because they are hard to keep off the agenda and will become more difficult to contain as they gain broader attention (Birkland 1997, p. 24).

Birkland's 1997 work was very important in that it discussed focusing events specifically and discussed their importance in getting items placed on the agenda. Birkland (2006) goes a step further. He studies the impact of focusing events not only on agenda setting, but on policy change. He argues that all policy makers go through a learning phase after a focusing event in order to learn how to handle the problem. He creates a model based on policy makers learning after a focusing event. He argues that learning is defined as "a process in which individuals apply new information and ideas or information and ideas elevated on the agenda by a recent event to policy decisions" (Birkland 1997, p. 22).

He argues that after an event all policy makers will say they are interested in ways to learn how to correct the problem. He does suggest that some policy makers will have less interest and less motivation to make changes to the current status quo because of ideological and organizational commitments (Birkland 1997, p. 17).

Second, he argues that not all focusing events carry the same weight, even those that are in the same field. One can have events that are discussed countrywide or regionally without causing much of a stir or one can have major events that really draw in the attention of the public and the media. He cites Columbine High School as a major focusing event that drew the attention of the entire country, after other shootings in Arkansas and Oregon in that same year had helped draw the attention to the problem of school violence (Birkland 1997, p. 163).

Third, interest groups mobilize. This mobilization draws more attention to those groups from the public, from the media, and from policy makers. Fourth, because of the mobilization and a desire for policy makers to learn, interest groups become far more prevalent, especially when it comes to legislative hearings.

Fifth, in order for there to be coherent policy created after a focusing event, there must be learning by policy makers. Birkland also argues that policy makers who are being pushed to do something by an alarmed public may pass policy that mimics another policy, or a policy that has been used elsewhere. What is particularly interesting is that Birkland is suggesting that policy makers sometimes make knee jerk reactions without much consideration of what the policy actually entails. This would indicate that in the short term following a focusing event, interest groups, and even powerful status quo ones, could have their interests trumped by an alarmed policy-making group (p. 20). Interestingly, Hayes (2001) also discusses this phenomenon and labels it *dramaturgical incrementalism.* He suggests that policy makers will react quickly to show the public that they are trying to handle the problem, but in fact the policy that is being created is solely symbolic. Symbolic policy is policy that is created to show the public that the government is doing something about the problem, though the policy may not receive funding or may be too difficult to enforce.

Sixth, much like Downs and his discussion of the issue-attention cycle, Birkland suggests that learning of policy makers decays over time. The interest in learning by policy makers, the media, and the public will wane and the suggestions and preferences become fewer. This corresponds with Downs, because it shows a gradual decline of interest in the creation of new policy by all actors involved. However, there can be a resurgence of interest in the policy realm if a new focusing event takes place. One can argue that the pre-problem stage and the post-problem stage of Down's attention cycle are actually the same stage. One happens before a given event and one takes place after, but in the firearms policy realm there are a series of focusing events that have taken place. Thus, a pre-problem stage for a future focusing event is actually the post-problem stage of a past focusing event.

Birkland (2006) applies his model to the cases of 9/11, airline security, and hurricane and earthquake disasters. The first problem he encounters with his model is that there are not many interest groups that were overly interested in what sort of changes were passed in each of these policy areas. Birkland also found that solutions to the problems were often already in the hands of policy makers in the form of briefings and reports. These solutions were often created by interest groups, specialists, and bureaucrats as solutions to focusing events that had happened in the past, but had failed to be implemented because of insufficient attention. In the cases Birkland used, the primary means of solutions were provided by specialists. Even though there had been reports on the potential problems for air security that became glaringly obvious on 9/11, there were also reports on how to fix these problems. Policy makers took the advice from specialists on how to implement the proposed solutions in the long term; however, Birkland also found that policy makers made knee-jerk policies after the event to show the public that they were in fact doing something.

Birkland's model stresses the importance of learning by policy makers, interest groups, and the media after a focusing event. He argues that not all focusing events are equal, but that each focusing event, even if it is small, is important because it does alert the public and the elites to a potential future problem. When a major focusing event occurs, interest groups are the primary educators of the public, the media, and policy makers. Interest groups, depending on their policy preference, will come up with different ways to handle the problem. These ideas on how to handle the problem are unlikely to be new, but are likely old solutions that they believe can be pushed forward during this period of opportunity (Birkland 2006, p. 86).

Unfortunately, because Birkland does not test his theory in an area where there are multiple adversarial interest groups, it is hard to understand whose policy ideas are heard and implemented and whose ideas are discarded, and why these ideas are either implemented or discarded. I would suggest that interest groups and the party in power play an important role in determining what kinds of ideas will be implemented. When there is a Republican-controlled legislature, then conservative interest groups will have their ideas implemented more readily than liberal interest groups. The opposite would also hold true. I also contend that when there are powerful status quo interest groups, that a rapid reaction will be less likely to become anything but symbolic because of the rapid damage control by the status quo group, and the ratcheting

up of pressure on its allies to prevent them from being swayed into passing knee-jerk policy.

In summary, focusing events occur suddenly, hitting everyone without
warning, affect a large number of people, and are rare. Further, the events
can affect the governmental agenda in profound ways because they can
lead to the redefinition of an issue and the attachment of powerful symbols to policy areas and policy learning by policy makers. Focusing events
are capable of getting agenda attention for an item, but interest groups
are capable of reacting quickly to contain (if a dominant status quo
group is present) or spread the issue (if a dominant pro-change group
is present). If a dominant status quo interest group or groups is present,
they should be able to slam the policy window shut before a policy goes
from the agenda stage to the formulation stage of the cycle. However,
if there is a dominant pro-change group or groups, they should be able
to use these policy windows, as Kingdon suggests, and drive new policy
from the agenda-setting stage to the formulation stage.

The literature has highlighted the key agenda-setting literature in the
United States, with a particular emphasis on focusing events. What we
can deduce is that focusing events are very important in bringing an
item to the public, media, and political consciousness. The literature
has also emphasized that policy entrepreneurs are very important in the
role of policy making when policy windows open. Policy entrepreneurs,
whether they are policy makers or interest groups, can promote or dissuade policy.

Canada: Agenda Setting

Soroka (2002) studies agenda-setting dynamics within Canada. He
argues that in order to understand agenda setting we must understand
the three types of agendas. He argues that there is a media agenda, a
public agenda, and a political agenda.

The media agenda is the political agenda of the Canadian mass media.
Soroka argues that the media itself has an agenda. He suggests that actors
who fall into the media agenda category are the news stations, influential
members within the media community, polling agencies, and people in
entertainment (Soroka 2002, p. 11).

The public agenda is measured by using a Gallup poll on the most
important problems in the country. However, Gallup Canada has not
been uniform in its question format and this has caused there to be

serious discrepancies in the data. This has in effect made public polling data in Canada very difficult to use (p. 47). This suggests that the public agenda in Canada may be hard to discern.

The Canadian policy agenda literature closely resembles the popular agenda-setting literature from the United States. But Soroka is quick to point out that the popular theories in agenda setting for the United States do not always apply to Canada (p. 55). The problem with applying American agenda-setting literature to Canada is discussed later in the chapter.

Soroka (2002) discusses various ways in which scholars have studied the policy agenda through government spending (p. 59). He argues that government spending is not always a good indicator of policy change because for the most part spending is incremental in nature (see also Wildavsky 1964).

In the United States legislative committees are widely studied for their importance. Committees in the United States are very important in their ability to kill bills. However, in Canada committees do not play nearly as important a role. Soroka (2002) argues that because of the minor role of committees, committee data should not be relied on heavily for proper results on agenda attention in Canada (p. 63). Other authors have also concluded the same (March 1974; Matheson 1976; Docherty 1997).

In Canada, executive speeches and press releases are not nearly as significant in presenting the position of the government as they are in the United States. The reason for this is because in the United States the president needs to gain public support and salience for his policies. In Canada, the prime minister and the cabinet have their hands directly on policy making and they do not need to inform the public well in advance of the policy proposals. The government initiates policy in cabinet and the policy is then announced by the appropriate minister in the House of Commons (Soroka 2002, p. 64).

However, the one executive release that Soroka finds to be of importance for understanding agenda setting in Canada is the Throne Speech. The functional equivalent of the Throne Speech is the State of the Union in the United States. The Throne speech provides an insight on the goals and preferences of the prime minister for that session of Parliament. These Throne Speeches often set the policy agenda for the country. The problem with Throne Speeches is that they do not come forth at any set interval. Throne Speeches are made at any new session of Parliament, which is generally an interval of time close to a year from the previous Throne Speech (Soroka 2002, p. 64).

Soroka also examines the relevance of studying legislation and legislative initiatives in relation to agenda setting. However, Soroka points out that many scholars will focus too heavily on legislation that has been implemented rather than all bills that were proposed yet failed to become legislation. He goes on to suggest that one of the biggest problems when studying Canadian legislation is that bills that are proposed by the government almost always become law, but bills that are proposed by individual legislators or private member's (PM) bills may be discussed, but rarely, if ever, become law. These bills rarely are taken seriously, and if they are considered, it is generally as symbolic legislation (Soroka 2002, p. 66).

Soroka suggests that one of the best ways to understand agenda setting and policy making in Canada is to listen to parliamentary debates, especially Question Period. Question Period in Canada, unlike in the United Kingdom where questions must be notified in advance, is totally spontaneous. This means that issues that are highly salient to the media and the public are readily and often brought before key policy makers (Soroka 2002, p. 69).

Now, it is important to examine how key agenda-setting literature from the United States holds up when applied to Canada. Howlett applies the theories of Kingdon's Garbage Can Model, Baumgartner and Jones' Punctuated Equilibrium, and Down's Issue Attention Cycle.

Howlett (1998) finds that policy windows similar to what Kingdon describes appear in other countries besides the United States. Howlett's study of the Canadian policy-making process includes several policy areas: acid rain, nuclear energy, capital punishment, and drug issues. Howlett defines and tests four types of policy windows (random, discretionary, spillover, and routine) on the aforementioned policies.

Random windows are just that, there is an unexpected policy opportunity that appears to come from nowhere. Howlett did not find any evidence of random windows, those which happen spontaneously, but he believes this is a product of the few cases that he studied in depth, and would not conclude that random windows never occur in Canada.

The second type of unpredictable policy window is the discretionary window. Here, politicians attempt to set the agenda to deal with a particular issue, normally selected from among matters already of some public concern (p. 506). He found the discretionary windows are often opened due to the media's influence. He found that discretionary windows were evident in Canadian policy making.

Spillover windows open when policy is created in one policy realm after policy has been created in a similar policy realm. Howlett suggests that a hypothetical spillover window may open when the government is considering acid rain policy; this may lead to the government also considering nuclear energy policy because both policy realms potentially deal with pollution and the environment. Howlett found some evidence that spillover windows do occur.

He also finds that the institutionalized nature of policy making in Canada leads to routine windows. He believes that these routine windows open more frequently during election years. This leads Howlett to suggest that routine windows open frequently and should be predictable, whereas at the other end of the spectrum there are the rare and random windows, and these are impossible to predict.

It is unlikely that the rare and random windows that Howlett discuss are in fact random. I would suggest that the presence of focusing events lead to the opening of these rare and random windows, which allows for policy makers and entrepreneurs to drive policy past the agenda-setting stage to the policy formulation, adoption, and implementation stage.

Howlett (1997) also studies the Down's Issue Attention Cycle and Punctuated Equilibrium by Baumgartner and Jones. Howlett uses a rigorous quantitative study of two policy areas, acid rain and nuclear energy, to test if the issue attention cycle plays a role in Canadian agenda setting. Howlett drew his data heavily from parliamentary records and major newspapers within Canada. When applying the Downsian model to agenda setting, he finds that it does not explain Canadian agenda setting very well. He argues that when applied to Canada, only circumstantial evidence can be found to support the Downsian model. When applying Punctuated Equilibrium to Canada, Howlett finds weak evidence that Punctuated Equilibrium exists in Canada. He suggests that this may be a coincidence more so than actual hard evidence. The reason for this, Howlett argues, is that when policy windows open it could be because of institutionalized reasons, such as elections or budget concerns, and not because of punctuations and events. Though Howlett appears to dismiss the impact of focusing events and argues that policy making in Canada is ordered, I argue that focusing events do matter in the gun control policy realm and that specifically in Canada; gun violence focusing events will carry a lot more weight in agenda setting and policy formulation.

When comparing agenda setting in the United States with Canada, we see some marked contrasts. An example of this is the minor role of committees in Canada, but their significance in the United States. However, there has been very rudimentary research on the impact of focusing events in Canada. Howlett is the closest in studying their impact, but appears to downplay the role of events. Ironically, Howlett argues that when policy windows do open, it is because of the ordered nature of institutions in Canada, yet, he also has great respect for Kingdon, who argues that the system is pure chaos and that because of this chaos, change is incremental. It is too difficult for policy makers to create vast and sweeping policy in a short time, thus they have to satisfice. I will apply Birkland's theory of focusing events to Canada in order to better understand the importance of events. Do they play a small role like Howlett argues, or do they in fact play a major role in getting items placed not only on the agenda, but into the formulation stage as well?

Summing Up the Literature: Agenda Setting

The majority of agenda-setting studies have been carried out in the United States. Baumgartner and Jones, Kingdon, and Birkland all are studying the impact of punctuations, garbage can models, and focusing events within the United States, and there is less emphasis in applying these frameworks to other states.

In Canada, scholars have applied some of the key American agenda-setting literature to events within Canada. Howlett specifically applies Downs, Kingdon, and Baumgartner and Jones. Howlett demonstrates that these theories can be applied cross-nationally, though the relevance of these theories to Canadian policy making may vary. Howlett tested the theories to only a few policies. In order for there to be a more robust study of agenda setting it is important to apply these theories to more policy areas. One theory Howlett did not test in the study of Canadian policy making is Birkland's studies of focusing events. For this study, I will be specifically studying the impact of focusing events within Canada.

In conclusion, focusing events in the United States have been found to draw the attention of the public and policy makers simultaneously. Focusing events, when coupled with mobilized interest groups seeking policy change, can lead to periods of change; however, the impact of focusing events can also be retarded by powerful status quo interest groups. Canadian scholars for the most part have ignored the impact of major events in shaking up the political environment in these states. It is important to understand how focusing events impact these two states in order to have a broader understanding of policy making there.

Interest Groups and Their Influence

Robert Dahl (1956), in his famous work, *A Preface to Democratic Theory*, brought up the issue of intense minorities and the role in which intensity might play in impacting policy making. Dahl defined intensity as "the degree in which an individual prefers some alternative." However, Dahl stated that this definition was lacking because it would be nearly impossible to distinguish just how much an individual really preferred that alternative (Dahl, p. 91). Nonetheless, Dahl outlined various situations in which an intense minority and an apathetic majority had opposing or concurrent preferences on an alternative. In all cases but one, Dahl stated that an intense minority and an apathetic majority would not cause any problem with democracy. However, there was one situation in which the intensity of the minority could provide a form of tyranny of the minority over the majority. In this situation the largest percentage of the majority only slightly favored the creation of a new policy; however, the majority of the intense minority was strongly opposed to the new policy. In this case, Dahl believed that the minority would be able to have tyranny over the majority and their policy alternatives would be created (Dahl, p. 99).

When looking at Dahl's description of when a minority has tyranny over the majority, we find that this scenario remarkably resembles the role that the NRA and its members have over the majority of apathetic Americans. Based on Dahl's assumption of intense minorities, the NRA is a prime example of when an intense minority can trump the interests of a majority that weakly favors gun control legislation.

In a similar realm of thought as Dahl, Schattschneider (1960) argues that in order to understand the power over policy change, we need to first understand the mobilization of bias. And in order to understand this, we need to know who is hampered by the mobilization of bias and who gains from it. He argues that in order to comprehend power, we need to know when there is non-decision making, that is when the status quo-oriented group or groups is able to influence the community not to make change or even consider making change. The NRA deliberately casts the gun control issue in moral terms to evoke the fundamental and personal values of gun owners (Spitzer 1988, p. 136; 1995). Finally, in order to understand decision making, the participation of individuals and groups needs to be taken into account.

Schattschneider (1960) makes a compelling argument about the mobilization of bias. He suggests that mobilized groups (interest groups) are able to limit decision making and that these groups are able to limit or deny new policy from being made. In relevance to this paper, this would suggest that after a focusing event, interest groups have the ability to prevent the creation of new policy.

Cobb, Keith-Ross, and Ross (1976) in their comparative study focus on mobilization of bias and the expansion of an issue. They argue that the public agenda items consist of three variables: (1) widespread attention, (2) action by a sizeable portion of the public, (3) attention to the item by an appropriate unit of government. An individual or a small group comes up with the agenda item, and then they try to expand the conflict. Opponents of the idea will try to contain expansion.

Cobb, Keith-Ross, and Ross (1976) identify three types of agenda setting: (1) outside initiative, (2) mobilization, and (3) inside initiative. Outside initiative is triggered by someone outside of government such as a nongovernmental group, whereas inside initiative is triggered by someone within the sphere of the government. Mobilization is when actors inside of government try to expand the issue from the formal agenda to the public agenda by garnering support. The authors believe that all three agenda-setting models can be found in any society. In egalitarian societies, the outside initiative model is more frequently used, in rich societies with central control; agenda setting is more likely to be caused by inside initiative. If a society is diverse and democratic, no particular style will be predominant.

In respect to interest groups and their role in various societies, Cobb, Keith-Ross, and Ross argue that groups are weak in material resources, but large in number are most successful using the outside initiative model. If a group is homogenous, they will mobilize more easily because the group is more likely to behave and think in a similar fashion. If a group represents lower economic groups, it is more likely to use the outside initiative model. If the group is used to support higher-level economic groups, it will more likely use the inside initiative model (see also Goldstein 1999).

Wilson and Herzberg (1987) find that the ability to block policy by a single individual or committee is a real possibility. The ability to block the agenda does not signify a specific outcome, but it does help protect the status quo. The ability to block legislation can be found in subcommittees, lower-level policy planners, and in the bureaucratic hierarchy. They argue that with so many groups having the ability to block legislation, it becomes very hard for there to actually be policy change. With the NRA being as powerful as any interest group, it is easy to understand how its influence could be felt at every step of the policy process.

Hall and Wayman (1990) find that moneyed interests are able to mobilize Congressional members who are already slanted to their ideological view of a given policy. They also find that when the moneyed interests lobby opponents, they have no effect.

Hall and Wayman find that moneyed interests are very capable of having a major impact on the outcome of a bill. They do so by mobilizing supporters in both the House and the Senate. They also try to mobilize swing legislators, those who do not have a strong position either way on a policy. They argue that it is possible that one moneyed interest's efforts will be balanced by an opposing moneyed interest lobbying efforts. The authors suggest that interest groups can counter each other when they are mobilizing Congressional members; however, the authors do not discuss the potential problem of the relative power of interest groups. Not all interest groups are created equal; this makes it possible for interest groups that have far more financial resources to outspend and thus outmobilize the competition. This would allow for interest groups to have more of a free reign in terms of mobilizing Congressional members for the creation or prevention of a policy.

Sinclair (1986) suggests that policy-oriented Congressional committees are very resistant to outside influences, but will make new public policy as long as the current trends match the ideology of the majority of the Congressional members on that committee. The author argues that hot button items such as banning abortion or school prayer were, in fact, counter to the views of the Democratic-controlled committees of the 1980s. She notes that it takes extreme pressure for political change from outsider actors (i.e. interest groups) actually to cause a committee to decide to make new public policy that is counter to their ideology.

Sinclair's argument demonstrates that structural arrangements of government can make it difficult to create new policy in the United States. She argued that Congressional members do in fact work closely with interest groups. This means that when there is a major focusing event, who is in power matters in determining whether new policy will be created or not. Allies to the gun lobby will be unlikely to support restrictions on firearms, whereas opponents to the gun lobby will be more inclined to support restrictions.

Pross (1986) argues that even though Canada has a pluralistic style of interest group representation it varies from the United States. He suggests that powerful interest groups that are institutionalized have very little problem accessing government through what he terms policy communities. Policy communities consist of interest groups who work closely with government, in particular bureaucratic agencies and that agencies minister (Pross 1986, p. 98). These communities also consist of the Parliament, outside interest groups that are both allies and rivals, and may even involve foreign governments and foreign interest groups. He suggests policy communities are more fluid than the iron triangle in the United States because of the lack of Congressional committees. However, the main actors in Canadian policy making are the dominant institutionalized interest group and the subsequent bureaucratic agency and cabinet (Pross 1986, p. 114).

Pross (1986) suggests that Canadian interest groups do not lobby in the same locations as their American counterparts. He finds that in Canada, 40% of all lobbying efforts are placed on the bureaucracy, 20% to back-benchers, 19% to the cabinet, and only 7% to legislative committees. In the United States, the bureaucracy is lobbied 21%, legislators 41%, the cabinet 4%, and legislative committees 19% of the time (pp. 58–9). This suggests that Canadians lobby some aspect of Parliament 46% of the time, but will lobby the bureaucracy nearly as often with 40%, but the United States 60% of lobbying efforts are directed at the Congress, and toward the bureaucracy only 21% of the time. This leads us to believe that in normal policy making the bureaucracy is lobbied far more heavily in Canada than in the United States. Also, counter to the argument furthered by Sinclair, legislative committees in Canada are far less important.

However, Pross provides data on where lobbying efforts are spent. He finds that lobbying efforts on laws are 51% of the time lobbied to the cabinet, and 11% to backbenchers, and only 19% to the bureaucracy. He also finds that 30% of all lobbying on bills is done to backbench-ers, 33% to the cabinet and once again only 19% to the bureaucracy (p. 58). Thus, Pross demonstrates that the bureaucracy is lobbied more in general, but Parliament actors are lobbied more often when it comes to matters such as bills and laws. This suggests that the Parliament is fundamentally important to interest groups who want to have favorable bills and legislation formulated, and the bureaucracy is less important to formulation.

If the major interest group and the majority of Congressional mem-bers are resistant to change, then no policy will be made. This is espe-cially true when considering the relationship between the NRA and the Republican Party (Spitzer 1988). Spitzer argues that because of this close relationship, which formally began in 1968 with the Republicans sup-porting firearms use and ownership in its party platform, the Republican

Party has become staunchly opposed to gun control. This close working relationship has enabled the NRA and the Republican Party to limit the amount of gun control legislation that has been created (Spitzer 1988, p. 104). Furthermore, if the policy community in Canadian policy making consists of groups that are resistant to change then it is likely policy will not be created there either. In recent years, we have seen that the NFA has not had nearly the success as the Coalition for Gun Control when considering the number of bills that have been created that favor stricter gun control legislation.

When we add in a discussion of interest groups with agenda setting, it is easy to see that they have a significant impact on policy. The two most important characteristics of interest groups are their ability to influence policy makers and their resources (political, organizational, and financial). The latter facilitates the former. As Pralle (2008) suggests, powerful, well-financed, well-organized interest groups are able to monopolize the time of policy makers, prevent venue shift, and are more adept at having their policy preferences enacted.

Pierson (2000) suggests that resources are a major factor in determining the success of an interest group. He argues that powerful advocacy groups can overwhelm their opponent and fill the political space opened up by a key event (Pierson 2000, p. 81). Groups that are financially powerful and can react quickly are much more adept at having their preferences implemented as policy.

Pross (1986) in his discussion of Canadian interest group organization states that interest groups must have a formal structure, clear definition of rules, a system of generating and allocating resources, a collective memory, rules for governing behavior, and most important procedures for reaching and implementing decisions (p. 113). He argues that institutionalized interest groups have all of these characteristics, which allows for them to be powerful over a long period of time. However, he suggests that single issue-oriented groups generally lack many of these key components, which generally results in them floundering and failing. He does suggest that single issue groups can become institutionalized. The Coalition for Gun Control in Canada seems to fit this typology. They came into being after the Montreal Massacre, but have had a lasting long-term impact.

Pralle (2008) argues that interest groups need not only be powerful, but they need to be able to handle venue shifts. Much like Schattschneider argues with expanding the conflict, Pralle argues that interest groups need to be able to focus their attack and resources at various levels of governance.

Pralle uses a case study of pesticide policy in the United States and Canada. She found that in the United States powerful pro-pesticide interest groups were capable of mobilizing and preventing the passage of new restrictive legislation. They were able to do this because they were far more organized than the opposition and they were able to mobilize at the local, state, and federal level. At the same time, antipesticide groups within the United States were very weak and disorganized and were unable to expand the conflict to other venues.

In Canada, the opposite held true. Antipesticide groups were far more powerful and far more organized than the pro-pesticide groups. The antipesticide groups realized that the pro-pesticide groups were more organized at the national level, so they shifted venues to ban pesticides to the provincial and local level. The pro-groups were unable to handle this venue shift because of lack of organization and resources. The antipesticide groups were able to have their preferences enacted (Pralle 2008).

Pralle's study demonstrates that the most powerful interest group in a certain policy area tends to trump rivals. Powerful interest groups are powerful because they are better organized, better financed, and better mobilized than their competitors. For this reason, in the United States the pro-pesticide group was able to be successful, but alternatively in Canada the antipesticide group was able to have their policy alternatives become law.

When we couple the interest group literature with the agenda-setting literature it paints, an interesting picture of the gun control policy realm. As noted above, policy entrepreneurs are very capable of promoting or preventing policy from going beyond the agenda-setting stage to the formulation stage. Policy makers will sometimes make quick reactions to focusing events, but according to Birkland (1997) and Hayes (2001) these policies are often symbolic.

Firearms-Related Interest Groups: The United States and Canada

The two most important interest groups in the United States that deal with the firearm debate are the NRA and the Brady Campaign. The NRA is the primary group that is pro-firearms and opposes most gun control legislation. Its rival is the Brady Campaign. The Brady Campaign actively attempts to limit the spread of firearms and has attempted to have restrictions placed upon them.

The NRA was formed in 1871. Its primary goal was to help train soldiers how to shoot with higher efficiency, after an abysmal showing by soldiers during the Civil War. The NRA's first foray into politics came in 1934 when the Legislative Affairs unit was created. However, the NRA did not directly lobby at this time; it wanted to keep its members abreast of gun control issues of the time (NRA.org).

The NRA did not become a true political entity until 1975 when the Institute for Legislative Action (ILA) was created. The ILA is the primary lobbying branch of the NRA. Since 1975 the NRA–ILA has become more and more active in gun control-related subjects in government (NRA.org).

On the opposite side of the gun debate is the Brady Campaign. The Brady Campaign was initially called Hand Gun Control Inc. Like many other interest groups that desire restrictive gun control legislation, it was founded after a focusing event. The Brady Campaign is named after James Brady, the Press Secretary for President Reagan who was shot during the attempted assassination of President Reagan in 1981. James Brady's wife started the group as a means to limit handguns; however, the Brady Campaign has become more all-encompassing, focusing on larger aims for gun control. The Brady Campaign is the primary opponent to the NRA.

In Canada, interest group behavior closely resembles that of their counterparts in the United States. Canada has a pluralist interest group structure. However, interest groups may not be nearly as powerful in Canada as they are in the United States. As Lijphart (1999) suggested earlier, parliamentary governments have strong centralized control of policy making, and minority parties and groups can be marginalized. This would lead us to predict that when there is a leftist government in power, leftist interest groups will be more likely to have their goals and preferences implemented, and right-wing interest groups will be less powerful at the national level. The opposite would also hold true, if there were a right-wing government in power, right-wing interest groups would be more likely to have their goals and preferences implemented. However, are interest groups goals and preferences turned into policy because of their lobbying efforts or because the party in power already has policy goals that are similar to the groups? By examining the case of gun control, we may be able to get a partial answer to this question. It is now important to take a look at the two most powerful interest groups that are centered on the gun debate in Canada: the NFA (the most powerful pro-firearm group) and the Coalition for Gun Control (the most powerful anti-firearm group).

In Canada, the NFA was formed in 1978. It has fought vigorously against what it deems to be unfair firearms legislation. Its primary purpose has been to further the idea of "fair and practical firearms legislation." Another of the major goals of the NFA is to help citizens and members of the NFA who have been accused of improperly possessing firearms. The NFA attempts to obtain legal counsel for these individuals, and have had great success in having some charges dropped. Mainly, the NFA has fought to protect what they deem to be their firearm rights and try to overturn the laws that were passed in the 1990s. They believe the passage of these laws were egregious violations of democratic values. Interestingly, these laws were passed after what is known as the Montreal Massacre (www.nfa.ca).

The Montreal Massacre led to the creation of the Coalition for Gun Control. They were created specifically because of that event. The Coalition states that it supports legislation that: requires permits for all guns, a cost-effective way to register guns, a total ban on all assault weapons, controls on all ammunition, and tighter restrictions in gun control (www. Guncontrol.ca).

It is clear that a single event, the Montreal Massacre, played a significant role in the creation of the Coalition for Gun Control, and it also led to the NFA becoming more politically motivated. What is interesting is that, based on Pralle's discussion of the power of interest groups, it would seem that interest groups that are already established would be better equipped at controlling an event; however, the NFA was unable to. A more in-depth study of the consequences of the Montreal Massacre is required to fully understand why the established NFA lost and why a new group won. In order to understand the role of gun violence focusing events on gun control policy in Canada, it is important to study not only the impact of just the Montreal Massacre, but other focusing events as well.

Canada: An Overview of Government Institutions

Earlier, I discussed the key differences between a presidential and parliamentary system. However, it is very important to go into a discussion of the specific institutions that are confronted with focusing events within Canada to get a complete picture. This section will discuss the Canadian Parliament and the role interest groups play in impacting the Canadian policy-making institutions.

Archer et al. (1999) describes the House of Commons as the "symbolic and physical centerpiece for Canadian policy making" (Archer 1999, p. 176). Currently there are 308 seats in the House of Commons. Each province and territory is approximately represented by its population. The largest province, Ontario, has one hundred and three seats while Prince Edward Island has four, the Northwest Territories two, and the Yukon but one (Archer 1999, p. 177).

The House of Commons is divided into two sections, with the ruling parties on one side and the opposition on the other. It is the duty and the responsibility of the opposition to criticize the policy making of the majority. This, in theory, should provide for lively debate and create better laws and legislation within Canada (Archer 1999, p. 182).

In Canada, there are several major parties that have influence at the federal level. These parties are: the Liberal Party, the Conservative Party, New Democratic Party, and the Bloc Quebecois. The Liberal Party and the Conservative Party are the most powerful, with each having had control of government various times in history. Unlike the United Kingdom where coalition government is rare, Canadian parties often have to unite in order to have a majority to control government (Archer et al. 1999). This means that it is harder for parties to drive through all of their policy preferences and have to be more willing and more capable of compromise in order to stay in power.

Party discipline plays a major role in parliamentary governments. Party discipline helps ensure that MPs support the cabinet and the prime minister. If party discipline is broached, it seriously jeopardizes the chance that an MP will later move up through the party ranks and can often lead to them becoming career backbenchers or being evicted from the party altogether. Interestingly, Archer et al. (1991) argue that party discipline does not have to be enforced by the leadership. In general, MPs will be loyal to the party because they are self-interested and want to move up through the ranks, and they also know that in order for them to have any lasting impression on the policy-making landscape in Canada, the party needs to gain power. And for the party to remain in power there has to be strict party discipline (Archer 1999, pp. 203–4).

The House of Commons is the primary source of legislative power within Canada. The previous discussion has demonstrated that government MPs in Canada usually will follow to the letter the goals of the cabinet and the prime minister. The strict party discipline that is seen in Canada is unlike anything seen in the United States, where

Representatives and Senators are more concerned with themselves and their constituents than their party.

Now that we have discussed in brief the House of Commons and party discipline it is important to look at the center of policy-making power within Canada: the prime minister and the cabinet. In 1867, Canada adopted cabinet government. Ministers within the cabinet are responsible to the House of Commons. Ministers are only able to serve as long as their party is in power. Ministers also are collectively responsible for their subordinates in their department. If subordinates do not carry out the goals of the cabinet, it is an embarrassment to the cabinet and the minister and can lead to the minister being forced to resign, though this has happened rarely. Ministers are also responsible to each other. They speak in unison to the public, to the rest of the House of Commons, and in the past to the Crown (Archer et al. 1999, p. 229).

Archer et al. (1999) argue that with the growth of party discipline, the strength of cabinet government has grown. They suggest that only through "gross mismanagement on the part of the government whip" could a cabinet lose on a piece of major legislation. The Canadian cabinet acts with the assurance that the rank and file members of the party will dutifully agree on legislation that has been proposed by it. The cabinet is almost completely in control of the wording of legislation; however, the passage of the legislation can be slowed both in the House and in the Senate (Archer 1999, p. 234). The Senate has formal powers to veto legislation; however, it has rarely used these powers to slow the creation of legislation (Archer 1999, p. 186). In the House, parliamentary committees have gained power in recent years and this has allowed for opponents to legislation to have some access in slowing the process (Archer 1999, p. 191).

The key figure within the cabinet is the prime minister. The prime minister is considered to be the first among equals (Archer 1999, p. 250). The prime minister is the elected party leader of the leading party. Party leaders have historically been nominated and selected at party conventions; however, in recent years there has been a shift to more direct elections for party leadership by party members (Archer 1999, pp. 469–70). The prime minister owes his or her position to the party and to the electorate, but not to cabinet ministers. In fact, the prime minister appoints the ministers; this means that even though the prime minister is supposed to be the first among equals, the prime minister should in fact have significant control over legislation created within the cabinet. Prime Ministers in Canada have also demonstrated the ability to stay in office for exceptionally long periods of time; this has allowed them to have a lasting impression on Canadian policy (Archer 1999, pp. 250–1).

The prime minister is the key official within the House of Commons. The prime minister is capable of influencing all members of the party within government to follow his lead on policy. Because of strict party discipline, the party will generally follow the lead of the prime minister. This gives the prime minister a more powerful relative position than the US president in that the prime minister will almost always have the complete support of the majority party.

The Canadian Senate is not nearly as powerful as its counterpart in the United States. The role of the Senate is to review the laws that have been passed by the House of Commons. The reason for this was initially intended to prevent excesses by the House and the prime minister and to provide sound technical review of the legislation (Archer 1999, p. 185).

If Senators do not approve of the legislation that has been passed in the House of Commons, they can veto it, and no override is present. As noted above, these formal powers have been used rarely by the Senate. The reason for this is likely due to the fact that Senators are not elected and are in fact appointed by the prime minister. However, because Senators are appointed for life, holdover members from the previous parties' reign in power can still be present when a new party takes over. When the former majority party of the House of Commons is still dominant in the Senate, the new party may have some difficulties, but as of this date, there have only been a few minor troubles between the House of Commons and the Senate. Thus, the Senate is more of an extension of the power of the prime minister, and is not nearly as important in policy making as the Senate in the United States.

Summing Up the Literature: Interest Group and Institutions

The US governmental institutions vary drastically from Canada. The presidential structure of the United States makes for a stark contrast to the parliamentary style of Canada. Though governmental institutions vary, both states have pluralist interest group structures. This suggests that interest groups will behave similarly in all three states, but because of the structure of governmental institutions, their influence may differ.

In the United States, governmental institutions are more diffuse, which allows for interest groups to have a multitude of access points to lobby the government. However, in parliamentary systems access points are fewer and further between because of the concentration of power in the lower houses. Interest groups are also less effective in lobbying individual members of Parliament because of strict party cohesion and the fact that members of Parliament rely on the party for power more than they will ever rely on an interest group.

Another important factor for interest groups in parliamentary governments is when parties opposed to the policy alternatives of that interest group are in power. In order to be successful, interest groups have to lobby cabinet members and the prime minister, but when these members of government are adversarial to the interest groups they will find that their influence is nearly eliminated.

In sum, I argue that interest groups will behave very much alike across borders, but because of governmental structure their influence will be dampened in parliamentary governments and increased in presidential states. In presidential systems there is often at least one chamber of the legislature or the Presidency that is controlled by a party that is favorable to an interest group's goals, but in parliamentary systems when a new government takes power interest groups will find that they either have new allies within government or have completely lost influence.

Theory

The literature demonstrates that there are a multitude of factors that impact agenda setting and formulation. Focusing events can lead to items being placed on the agenda. Interest groups play a significant role by encouraging the placement of items on the agenda or the denial of items on the agenda. Focusing events, when coupled with interest groups can lead to policy change or the prevention of policy change.

Looking comparatively at agenda setting, we find that the structure of governments plays a significant role in determining if a policy will be placed on the agenda and if policy will advance to the formulation stage. The party in power also plays a role in determining how policy changes after a focusing event, but is not as significant as interest groups or the structure of government in determining the eventual outcome of policy.

In the United States interest groups should be able to impact the formulation of policy after a focusing event because of access. Interest groups are able to influence individual legislators, and they have multiple government institutions that they can influence. In parliamentary systems, such as Canada, interest group impact is marginalized by the lack of access due to the concentrated power of the executive and legislative branch, the absence of access points, and an inability to influence individual legislators.

Another important factor in considering interest groups is that, on any given issue, there can be a pro-change group and/or a pro-status quo group. However, just because there is the presence of at least one of these different types of interest groups does not mean that they are equal. On any given issue, one group may be more powerful in a variety of ways (membership, funding, and organization) than the other. This power helps these interest groups in creating or preventing change due to a focusing event. In pluralist systems, when there is a dominant interest group, it will have significant sway over the formulation of policy. If the dominant interest group is a status quo group, it will be able to prevent the formulation of new policy; however, if the dominant interest group is a pro-change group, it may be able to facilitate the formulation of new policy.

The second major factor in determining whether a focusing event will impact policy is the structure of governments in a given state. The United States has a presidential system where Canada has a parliamentary system. States that are presidential have a diffusion of power (power is not concentrated in one branch of government). This causes a slowing of the policy-making process and results in natural delays.

In parliamentary systems, the power of the government tends to be concentrated in one branch of government. This can lead to the quick passage of new policy when there is a focusing event. Parliamentary systems can pass policy quickly and efficiently before there has been a cooling-off period for policy makers, interest groups, and the public.

The third factor considered is the party that is in power. When the Republican Party is in control of the Presidency and the Congress, gun violence focusing events will not lead to any new federal gun control laws. In the case of divided government in the United States, the gridlock that comes from it will make it very difficult for either party to pass new legislation. When the Democratic Party is in control of the Presidency and the Congress, slight to no changes will be made to federal gun control law after a focusing event. In Canada, when right-wing parties are in power gun violence focusing events can lead to incremental change, but when leftist parties are in control broad and sweeping legislation could be passed. Conservative, right-wing governments in Canada will behave similar to what Walgrave et al. (2008) proposed. That being, during times of heightened public awareness to the gun control issue, and pressures from pro-gun control interest groups, they will pass policy that does not necessarily coincide with their party platform. However, I theorize, that because these governments are more conservative, they will be less inclined to make sweeping changes to policy than their left-wing counterparts.

Major Themes of the Book

With the above discussion in mind, it is important to lay out and discuss the major themes of the book that are answered in the next few chapters. The first and most important theme of the book deals with the issue of responsiveness to gun violence focusing events. The United States is far less responsive to the creation of new restrictive gun control laws than Canada. Chapter 3 discusses the importance of a presidential system, interest groups, political parties, and public opinion on the formulation of gun control in the United States. Chapter 3 discusses the significance of a parliamentary government, interest groups, political parties, and public opinion in the formulation of gun control in Canada after a focusing event. Thus, Chapters 3, 4, and 5 attempt to answer the question: Why is the United States less responsive to gun violence focusing events than Canada, and which factors are the most important?

In Chapter 3, several of the themes that are discussed provide helpful insight into answering the primary theme of the book. In the United States, the NRA is the most powerful group that exists in the gun control policy subsystem. The NRA is a staunchly status quo group that resists restrictive gun control laws. The NRA has long been a close ally of the Republican Party. For this reason, it is logical that when the Republicans are in control of government, or when there is divided government (those periods of time when the Republicans control at least one branch of the Congress or the Presidency) restrictive gun control policy will never be made at the best of times. Thus, when there are major gun violence focusing events they may drive the issue of gun control to the agenda, but rarely will these events lead to new gun control policy because of the NRA and its allies in Congress.

Another major theme researched in Chapter 3 is when the Democrats have unified control over government. It could be assumed that when the Democrats have unified control over policy making that gun control policy would be created relatively easily, especially when there are focusing events. It is true that the major pieces of restrictive gun control legislation that have been created were created under unified Democrat control; however, none of this legislation was created easily nor was it comprehensive. And this was due to the NRA and its allies. After the election of 1994, I would argue that Democrats are even more reluctant to touch upon the gun control issue. Thus, even when the Democrats have unified control over the policy-making process, gun control policy will rarely be created, and when it is, will be incremental (or incomprehensive) in nature, and after the 1994 election, may never be created again because of the NRA and its Republican allies.

In Chapter 4, I discuss Canada and how it handles the creation of gun control policy after major focusing events. In the United States, the NRA, a staunchly status quo group reigns supreme; however, in Canada, the Coalition for Gun Control, a staunchly anti-firearm group is the most influential interest group in the gun policy realm. The Coalition for Gun Control was not created until the Montreal Massacre. Because of this, my study primarily focuses on gun control policy in Canada that was created after the birth of this group.

In Canada, when there is a major focusing event and a left-of-center party or parties control policy making, there can be major overhauls to gun control policy. These left-of-center parties tend to work with the Coalition for Gun Control and are very reluctant to be influenced by pro-gun groups. Thus, in Canada, when there is a major focusing event, and leftist parties control government, gun control policy can be made quickly, efficiently, and the legislation created can lead to significant changes.

Interestingly, when right-of-center parties control government in Canada, and major gun violence focusing events take place, gun control legislation can still be created. Right-of-center parties do appear to be more reluctant to create legislation; however, the pressure placed upon them by the Coalition for Gun Control and oftentimes by members of their party, in particular women (due to the feminist context to the gun control movement in Canada), restrictive gun control laws are still created after major events. Thus, even when right-of-center parties control the policy-making process in Canada, restrictive gun control laws can still be made.

Methods of Research

In order to test the themes of the book, I used a case-study approach of each state. The primary gun violence focusing events that took place in each state are identified and then analyzed. In order to understand the impact of each individual focusing event on gun control policy, it will be important to find a linkage between the focusing event and policy being placed on the federal government agenda and policy formulation. There has been circumstantial evidence discussed above that suggests that focusing events do lead to new policy in Canada, and that focusing events have a minimal effect in the United States except when there is a left-of-center government.

First, I used public opinion polls. I used these opinion polls for a variety of reasons. First, it allowed for me to understand what the public's opinion was on gun control policy throughout my time period. Second, these public opinion polls provide a solid understanding of whether or not a gun culture really existed and had this gun culture been increased or dwindled over time.

Second, I analyzed all gun bills that were proposed by Congress between 1963 and 2008 and government bills proposed by the Parliament between 1989 and 2008. In particular, I was interested in finding variation in the number of bills proposed and bills passed during Congresses or Parliaments that contained focusing events when compared to those that did not. By analyzing these bill proposals it allowed me to demonstrate how government institutions and interest groups are capable of influencing agenda attention and policy outcomes.

Third, I cross-referenced press releases, of the *New York Times* in the United States, and the *Globe and Mail* in Canada. These newspapers helped me confirm that the focusing events discussed were in fact major focusing events. They were able to do this because they are national newspapers that discuss events at the national level. Some gun violence events may have local and state significance, but are less important on the national level. These newspapers also allowed for me to analyze the data from the day of the event, until the event was no longer mentioned in the newspaper. This demonstrated that the event had become less important to the media, and demonstrated a gradual decline of public interest to the event. The data taken from the newspaper demonstrated the importance of the event and also allowed for an understanding of what form of immediate response lawmakers had to the event. I was also interested in discovering how interest group leaders addressed the event through interviews given by them to the media. I covered the newspaper coverage of new gun control legislation. When new policy was created it is important to understand that new policy was created in response to a particular focusing event and what lawmakers and interest groups thought of the new gun control legislation.

Chapter 3

The United States: Violence Leads Nowhere

General Gun Control Attitudes and Opinions

This section covers public attitudes on gun control policy. The data was compiled by the *Pollingreport.com*. The *Pollingreport.com* is a web service that compiles public opinion data from many sources into a single, easily to access web sheet. The majority of the data collected on public attitudes dates from the 1990s to 2008. Older public opinion polls were harder to obtain.

The first opinion poll was collected by the Gallup from 1990 to 2008. The question posed by the poll was: Do you feel that the laws covering the sale of firearms should be made more strict, less strict, or kept as they are now? (see Table 3.1).

The data collected from this poll demonstrates that public attitudes on firearms controls had changed in 18 years. In 1990, 78% of the public sought stricter gun control laws, whereas only 2% sought more lenient laws, and 17% of the population thought that laws should be kept as they are now. However, the data demonstrates that there was actually a downward trend in attitudes that seek stricter laws and an increase in attitudes that sought lenient laws or the law being kept as they were. The 2008 poll demonstrates that only 49% of the population sought stricter gun control laws, whereas 8% sought lenient laws and 41% wanted the laws to stay the same as they are were.

ABC News/*Washington Post* poll used a similar survey from 1999 to 2009. The question posed was: Do you favor or oppose stricter gun control laws for this country? (see Table 3.2).

The public opinion data showed a range of 57–67% of the population favoring stricter gun control legislation, except in 2009 when only 51% favored stricter gun control legislation. When comparing and contrasting the data taken from these two polls, we can see some discrepancy in public attitudes. For example, there had been a downward trend of those who favored stricter gun control legislation in the Gallup poll and

Table 3.1   Do you feel that the laws covering the sale of firearms should be made more strict, less strict, or kept as they are now?

	More strict (%)	Less strict (%)	Kept as now (%)	Unsure (%)
Oct./3–5/2008	49	8	41	2
Oct./4–7/2007	51	8	39	2
Oct./9–12/2006	56	9	33	2
Oct./13–16/2005	57	7	35	1
Oct./11–14/2004	54	11	34	1
Jan./9–11/2004	60	6	34	—
Oct./6–8/2003	55	9	36	—
Oct./14–17/2002	51	11	36	2
Oct./11–14/2001	53	8	38	1
May/5–7/2000	62	5	31	2
Apr. 2000	61	7	30	2
Dec. 1999	60	10	29	1
Aug. 1999	66	6	27	1
June 1999	62	6	31	1
May 1999	65	5	28	2
Apr. 1999	66	7	25	2
Feb. 1999	60	9	29	2
Apr. 1995	62	12	24	2
Dec. 1993	67	7	25	1
Mar./12–14/1993	70	4	24	2
Mar./21–24/1991	68	5	25	2
Sept./10–11/1990	78	2	17	3

Source: Gallup poll (1990–2008).

this trend was not nearly as pronounced in the ABC News/*Washington Post* poll. However, the main point that should be taken from these data is that in virtually every year at least 50% of the population has favored stricter gun control legislation. In a majority of years at least 60% of the public favored stricter gun control laws. However, public opinion has not translated into new restrictive gun control laws.

Handgun Attitudes and Opinions

The first public opinion poll discussed in this section was collected by Gallup from 1959 to 2008. The question posed was: Do you think

Table 3.2 Do you favor or oppose stricter gun control laws for this country?

	Favor (%)	Oppose (%)	Unsure (%)
Apr. 2009	51	48	1
Apr. 2007	61	36	3
Oct. 2006	61	37	2
May 2002	57	37	6
Jan. 2001	59	39	2
May 2000	67	30	3
Apr. 2000	64	34	2
Sept. 1999	63	35	2
Aug. 1999	63	34	3
May 1999	67	31	1

Source: ABC News/*Washington Post* (1999–2009).

there should or should not be a law that would ban the possession of handguns, except by the police and other authorized persons? (see Table 3.3).

The data in this graph did not include all firearms and did not include all of the years of my study, but they do include one of the most controversial gun types: handguns. The data provided us with some surprising results. The only time in the history of my study that more people favored a handgun ban rather than opposed a handgun ban was 1965, when 49% of the population favored gun control whereas 44% opposed gun control. Of the other years analyzed in this poll, the lowest percentage of people to oppose handgun bans was 50% of the population, and in the majority of the data collected after 1993, better than 60% of the population opposed handgun bans. Even when there was the presence of major focusing events such as in 1981, 1999, and 2007, the highest percentage of people to favor handgun bans was 38% in 1999, and the lowest percentage of those who opposed handgun bans was 54%.

Other polls have focused on similar handgun issues. Pew Research Center for the People and the Press conducted a poll between 1993 and 2008. The poll posed the question: Would you favor or oppose a law that banned the sale of handguns? (see Table 3.4).

Like the data collected from the Gallup poll, the data collected by the Pew Research Center for the People and the Press demonstrated

Table 3.3 Do you think there should or should not be a law that would ban the possession of handguns, except by the police and other authorized persons?

	Should be	Should not be	No opinion
Oct. 2008	29	69	2
Oct. 2007	30	68	2
Oct. 2006	32	66	2
Oct. 2005	35	64	1
Oct. 2004	36	63	1
Oct. 2003	32	67	1
Oct. 2002	32	65	3
Aug. 2000	36	62	2
Apr. 1999	38	59	3
Feb. 1999	34	64	2
Dec. 1993	39	60	1
Mar. 1993	42	54	4
Mar. 1991	43	53	4
Sept. 1990	41	55	4
July 1988	37	59	4
Oct. 1987	42	50	8
June 1981	41	54	5
Apr. 1981	39	58	3
Dec. 1980	38	51	11
Jan. 1980	31	65	4
1975	41	55	4
1965	49	44	7
1959	60	36	4

Source: Gallup poll (1959–2008).

Table 3.4 Would you favor or oppose a law that banned the sale of handguns?

	Favor (%)	Oppose (%)	Unsure (%)
Apr./23–27/2008	36	59	5
Apr./18–22/2007	37	55	8
Mar./15–19/2000	47	47	6
Sept. 1999	46	50	4
May 1999	44	50	6
Dec. 1993	45	51	4

Source: Pew Research Center (1993–2008).

Table 3.5 Would you favor stricter or less strict laws relating to the control of handguns?

	May 2000 (%)	June 1999 (%)	Apr. 1998 (%)
Stricter	72	73	76
Less strict	20	20	19
Neither	6	5	5
Don't know	2	2	–

Source: Harris poll (1999–2000).

Table 3.6 Would you favor or oppose the registration of all handguns?

	Favor (%)	Oppose (%)
2000	73	26
1999	79	19
1993	81	18
1991	80	17
1990	81	17
1985	70	25

Source: Gallup poll survey (1985–2000).

that the majority of the public had been against the outright banning of handguns. However, this did not mean that the majority of the public opposed stricter handgun control measures. The Harris Poll in a three-year study asked the question: In general, would you say you favor stricter or less strict laws relating to the control of handguns? (see Table 3.5).

This Harris poll demonstrated that there was a stark difference between opinions regarding the banning of handguns versus opinions that favored stricter regulation of handguns. This demonstrated that the public did not favor outright bans on handguns, but they did in fact desire the creation of more gun control measures.

A Gallup poll survey that was periodically taken from 1985 to 2000 asked whether or not the public would favor the registration of all handguns. The results demonstrated that an overwhelming percentage of US citizens do, in fact, support the registration of all handguns (see Table 3.6).

In general, the public opinion data in this section has shown us that the majority of Americans do favor restrictions on handguns. In particular, the registration of all handguns was heavily favored throughout the polls. However, Americans are heavily against the banning of handguns. This suggests that most Americans appear to be willing to find a middle ground when it comes to handgun ownership.

Assault Weapon Attitudes and Opinions

Assault weapons, those weapons that are fully automatic or semiautomatic, have long been a contention in the battle over gun control policy in the United States. The Assault Weapons Ban was created in 1994 and banned a specific set of assault weapons. This ban expired in 2004. There were a number of polls that sought the American public's attitude toward these assault weapons and bans on them.

In 1999, an ABC News/*Washington Post* poll asked: Would you oppose or support a ban on the sale of all assault weapons? Of the 1,526 adults polled, 77% said they would favor the ban, and only 22% said that they would oppose the ban.

In 2000, a similar poll was taken by CBS News/*New York Times*. The poll asked: Do you favor or oppose the nationwide ban on assault weapons. Of the 947 adults polled, 68% favored the ban, where only 28% opposed the ban.

In 2003, a poll by NBC News/*Wall Street Journal* asked: About ten years ago Congress banned the sale of assault weapons. In your view, should Congress keep or end this ban. Of the 1,003 adults polled, 78% favored keeping the ban and only 16% thought the ban should end.

In 2004, the Harris poll conducted a similar poll. The question posed was: Do you favor continuing the ban (of assault weapons)? Of the 1,018 people polled, 71% favored keeping the Assault Weapons Ban, and only 26% opposed the ban.

These four polls provide useful insight on the attitudes of Americans on the ban on assault weapons from 1999 to 2004. Even though the polls were taken at different times, and by different polling services the results were clear: Americans tend to favor the banning of assault weapons.

ABC News/*Washington Post* conducted a multi-year poll asking the public if they would favor a ban on assault weapons. The results in this poll reaffirm the results of the earlier polls. The public tends to favor the banning of assault weapons (see Table 3.7).

Table 3.7 Would you favor a ban on assault weapons?

	Support (%)	Oppose (%)	Unsure (%)
Apr./22/2007	67	30	3
May/2000	71	27	2
Sept./1999	77	22	1
May/1999	79	19	2
June/1994	80	18	2

Source: ABC News/*Washington Post* (2007).

The Assault Weapons Ban was created in 1994, and as of 2008, nearly four out of every five Americans favored the banning of assault weapons. When the Assault Weapons Ban was allowed to expire in 2004, there was still overwhelming support for it. This suggests that public opinion, even when it overwhelmingly supports a ban on assault weapons, can be trumped by policy makers and interest groups. As mentioned earlier in the work, powerful interest groups and their ability to influence policy makers can trump the opinion of the masses when it comes to the policy making. The decline of the Assault Weapons Ban coupled with the data from these polls provides excellent evidence for this point.

The examination of the public opinion on gun control in the United States demonstrates that public opinion has consistently favored more restrictive gun controls. However, in general terms, the desire to create more restrictive gun control by the general public has not led to new gun control laws. Thus, it would appear that public attitudes have very little impact on the creation of new gun control laws in the United States.

Latter portions of this chapter describe other factors which influence the creation or prevention of gun control laws. In Chapter 5, American public attitudes on gun control are compared and contrasted with Canadian public attitudes on gun control.

Preview on Congressional Attention to Gun Bills

This section studies bill proposals and their outcomes from 1963 to 2008. The main goal of this section is to determine the importance of focusing events to agenda attention, Congressional activity, and gun control policy. The data in this section also analyzes the role in which political parties are able to promote or retard gun control legislation.

The data was collected from the Congressional Index, and from the Electronic Congressional Index found on *Thomas.gov*. While searching the Congressional Index, I did an overall count of all bills proposed in a Congressional session, but I also examined each bill proposal in order to understand if the bill that was introduced was a restrictive bill or a lenient bill.

A restrictive bill was categorized by being a bill that made present gun control policy more restrictive in some fashion, such as making waiting periods, taxing ammunition, banning certain firearms, etc. A lenient bill was categorized by being a bill that made gun control policy more lenient in some fashion, such as providing exemptions, repealing laws, etc. Some bills that were proposed were not considered to be either restrictive or lenient and were removed from the analysis. Generally, these bills were the ones that involved stricter penalties for offenders who used firearms during the commission of a crime. These bills were discarded because even though they make criminal laws more restrictive, they were almost always proposed by Congressional members who favored lenient gun control laws. Thus, they are laws that target criminals and aren't laws that target guns and were excluded.

Major Gun Violence Focusing Events

Before discussing the impact focusing events have on agenda attention, it is important to identify the focusing events that were used in the book. I identified nine major focusing events, some of which were assassinations or assassination attempts, others were mass murders. These focusing events were the ones that received the most attention on the national level by the *New York Times* and made politicians and interest groups question whether new federal gun control legislation should be created or not. These events are also the ones that were still being cited as examples of major gun violence years later. I realize that there have been other gun violence events, but these other events did not merit the attention nationally and politically as the ones listed in Table 3.8.

As noted above there are two basic types of major gun violence events: assassinations and mass murders. Though these events differ in scope and target, the policy reaction by politicians and interest groups tend to be the same to each type of event. What I mean by this, if hypothetically, an assault weapons ban or a waiting period had been sought by gun control proponents before an event, it would not matter if it were an

Table 3.8 Major gun violence focusing events, 1963–2008

Year	Focusing event	Party in control of House of Representatives	Party in control of Senate	Party of President
1963	JFK assassination	Democrat	Democrat	Democrat
1968	RFK assassination	Democrat	Democrat	Democrat
1968	Martin Luther King assassination	Democrat	Democrat	Democrat
1981	Attempted assassination of Reagan	Democrat	Republican	Republican
1989	Stockton massacre	Democrat	Democrat	Republican
1991	Killeen Texas massacre	Democrat	Democrat	Republican
1999	Columbine School shooting	Republican	Republican	Democrat
2007	Virginia Tech shooting	Democrat	Democrat	Republican

assassination or a mass murder, the bill that was being sought by these proponents would still be the same. I also argue that the response by gun groups that sought the status quo would also be similar. Thus, whether the event was an assassination or a mass murder doesn't matter to agenda attention in my analysis.

Trends in Gun Bill Proposals Overtime

This section of the book examines gun bill proposals. Each gun violence focusing event that was listed above is displayed in the figures that follow. This allows for an examination of the data to determine if increases in gun bill proposals are impacted by focusing events. Throughout Chapter 3, I break the gun control data into categories based upon Congressional session and not year. Because of this trend, especially later on in this chapter, is why I use Congressional sessions on the *x*-axis of the graphs given in the figures in this section. Figures 3.1 and 3.2 examine the House and Figures 3.3 and 3.4 examine the Senate.

Figures 3.1 and 3.2 examine House gun bill proposals overtime: the first examines all bills proposed and the second categorizes gun bill proposals by whether they were lenient or restrictive.

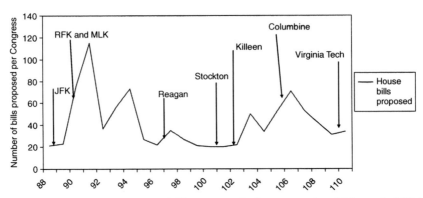

FIGURE 3.1 House firearm bills proposals between the 88th and 110th Congress (1963–2008)

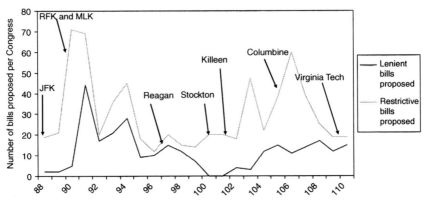

FIGURE 3.2 Trends in House firearms bills proposals between the 88th and 110th Congress (1963–2008)

Figures 3.1 and 3.2 show that between the 88th and 95th Congress, 1963–78, there were a large number of gun bills being proposed. The number of gun bills proposed leveled out between the 96th and the 103rd Congresses, 1979–92. However, from the 103rd Congress until the 108th Congress, 1993–2003, the number of gun bills being proposed once again increased significantly.

On examining the figures, we notice that a couple of trends begin to emerge. The first is gun violence focusing events have an impact on House gun bill proposals. After the John F. Kennedy assassination the number of all types of House gun bills being proposed increased significantly; however, after the assassinations of Robert Kennedy and Martin

Luther King Jr, the number of House gun bills proposed reached its highest point. After the 1968 Gun Control Act, was formulated and implemented during the 90th Congress, the number of restrictive House bills proposed decreased significantly while the number of lenient bills proposed reached their highest point. Gun bill proposals stayed at a fairly low rate even after the attempted assassination of Reagan. After the Stockton and Killeen massacres there was a lagged effect of two Congresses in the House before there was a marked increase in restrictive gun bills proposals. However, starting with the 103rd Congress, 1993–94, the number of House gun bills being proposed increased significantly.

The second trend that is noticed is the party of the president and its impact on determining gun bill proposals. The Stockton and Killeen shootings took place when there was a Republican President; however, the increased number of gun bills proposed coincided with a Democrat President being elected to office. After the passage of two restrictive pieces of legislation during the 103rd Congress, 1992–93, and the massive defeats the Democrats took in the House in 1994, the number of restrictive gun bills proposed went in to decline and the number of lenient bills being proposed increased significantly. The number of restrictive gun control bills being proposed had a brief resurgence after the Columbine slayings, but the number of lenient gun control bills being proposed continued to be at their highest since the late 1960s.

Figures 3.1 and 3.2 indicate that gun violence focusing events impact gun bill proposals in the House. The number of bills proposed is greatly impacted by focusing events; however, the party in power of the House and maybe even more importantly the party of the president are also very important in dictating the number and type of House bills proposed.

Figures 3.3 and 3.4 examine Senate gun bill proposals overtime: the first examines all bills proposed and the second categorizes the gun bill proposals by whether they were lenient or restrictive.

Trends in Senate gun bill proposals closely resemble the trends seen in the House. After the three major focusing events of the 1960s, the John F. Kennedy assassination in 1963, and the Robert Kennedy and Martin Luther King assassinations in 1968 there was a large increase in Senate bill proposals. In particular there was a spike in restrictive gun control legislation. After the 1968 passage of the Gun Control Act, restrictive Senate bill proposals declined and lenient bill proposals increased significantly. This trend is also seen in the House.

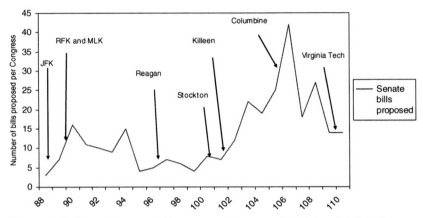

FIGURE 3.3 Senate firearms bills proposed between the 88th and 110th Congress (1963–2008)

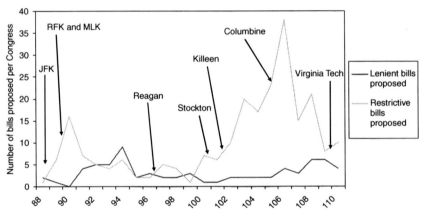

FIGURE 3.4 Trends in Senate firearms bills proposed between the 88th and 110th Congress (1963–2008)

The number of Senate gun bill proposals of both types decreased significantly from the 95th Congress to the 101st Congress, 1977–89. In the 101st Congress, we saw the Stockton Massacre which was followed by the Killeen Texas slayings in the 102nd Congress. These two events coincided with a significant increase in restrictive Senate gun control proposals. The number of restrictive Senate bills continued to increase throughout the 1990s when there was a Democrat as president. The only time there was a slight decrease in this trend was during the 104th Congress when the Republicans gained control of the House. The largest number of total and restrictive bills proposed transpired after the Columbine school shooting during the 106th Congress, 1999–2000. However, after a Republican was elected to the Presidency in 2000, the number of restrictive Senate bills proposed once again dropped significantly.

The data in Figures 3.1–3.4 demonstrates that gun bill proposals appear to be driven by the presence of focusing events. Agenda attention to focusing events is also impacted by the party of the president. When there is a Republican President, restrictive gun bill proposals are much lower than when there is a Democrat President. In order to better understand how parties and the president impact gun bill proposals, the next section of this chapter breaks down bill proposals into several categories which are discussed below.

Bill Proposals and Agenda Attention to Gun Control Policy

The next portion of this chapter breaks down bill proposals into four separate categories. These categories examine bill proposals by overall numbers of bills proposed, bills proposed during Congresses that contained a major focusing event, bills proposed in post-focusing event Congresses, and bills proposed in Congresses that did not have a major focusing event and did not follow a post-focusing event Congress. I use this technique in breaking down the data because it allows for a better determination of the impact of focusing events and the impact of allowing for a lagged response by policy makers in introducing new gun control legislation.

Figures 3.5 and 3.6 examine all bill proposals between 1963 and 2008: the first examines the House and the second examines the Senate.

Figures 3.5 and 3.6 in this section encompass all the data that was gathered on the House and the Senate. When we examine the House, we can see that the number of bills being introduced after a focusing event actually declines when compared to the overall numbers; however, the biggest change is that the number of lenient bills decreases by nearly 50%, and there is actually a small increase in restrictive bills being proposed. This trend, the number of lenient House bills being proposed declining during a Congress that contains a focusing event, is seen more often than not throughout the data. It suggests that there may be a concern for legislators that their attempts to create lenient laws would appear

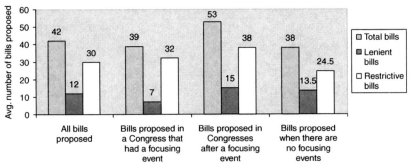

FIGURE 3.5 Average number of House bills proposed (1963–2008)

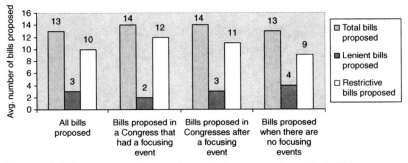

FIGURE 3.6 Average number of House bills proposed (1963–2008)

insensitive to the public, media, and interest groups. However, in post-focusing event Congresses, the number of restrictive House bills and lenient House bills introduced are both higher than the average. This is because after there has been a cooling-off period both sides of the issue are ready to wage battle. Thus, in post-focusing event Congresses you will find the most contention. Finally, not surprisingly, when there are no major focusing events, there is a large decrease in restrictive House bills being proposed, but lenient bills being proposed are at their second highest, following only post-focusing event Congresses. This signifies that lenient bill proponents try to have legislation created when gun control policy is not a salient issue, which it becomes after a focusing event.

When we turn to the Senate, we notice that there is not much variation when we scrutinize the four categories. There is a slight increase in restrictive gun bills and a slight decrease in lenient gun bills being proposed when there is a major focusing event. There is also more lenient gun bills proposed and less restrictive gun bills proposed than at any other time when there are no major focusing events. However, the change is so slight from one category to the next it is hard to state that these trends are directly attributed to focusing events, and could rather be due to random variation.

Because the numbers in these two categories are all encompassing and do not allow us to examine the data based on party or president, I found it important to delve deeper into the data. Figures 3.7 and 3.8 examine gun bill proposals when there is a Democrat-controlled Congress. These are followed by Figures 3.9 and 3.10 that examine gun bill proposals when there is a Republican-controlled Congress.

The data listed above only encompasses data in which there was a majority of Democrats in that chamber. When we examine the House data, we find that after a focusing event the number of total bills proposed

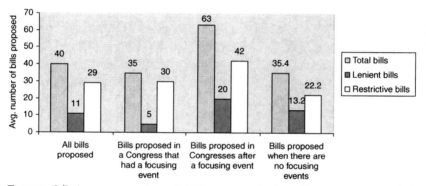

FIGURE 3.7 Average number of bills proposed when Democrats control the House (1963–2008)

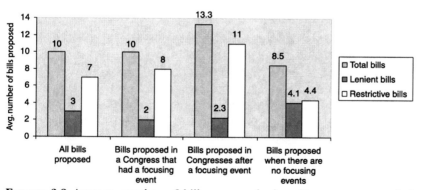

FIGURE 3.8 Average number of bills proposed when Democrats control the Senate (1963–2008)

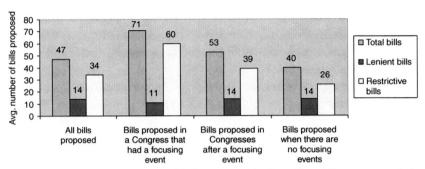

FIGURE 3.9 Average number of bills proposed when Republicans control the House (1963–2008)

declines; however, the number of restrictive bills proposed increases, with the biggest change being the number of lenient bills dropping considerably. Like we see in the general trends discussed in the first part of this section, the biggest battle ground for bill proposals is during post-focusing event Congresses. The total number of bills proposed, the total number of lenient bills proposed, and the total number of restrictive bills proposed are all at their highest. Lastly, the number of bills proposed when there are no major focusing events demonstrates that restrictive bill proposals are at their lowest and lenient bills are at their second highest. When we look at bill proposals when there is a Democrat House, we find the same trends we saw when we examined overall House bill proposals: (1) a decline of lenient bill proposals when there is a focusing event; (2) a huge number of lenient and restrictive bills being proposed in post-focusing event Congresses; and (3) the number of restrictive bills being proposed declining significantly when there are no major focusing events present.

Figure 3.8 examines the Senate when it was controlled by the Democrats. The data shows that when there is a major focusing event the number of restrictive Senate bills proposed increased slightly, and the number of lenient bills proposed decreased slightly. Like in the House, the largest number of restrictive bills being proposed occurred in post-focusing event Congresses; however, unlike the House the number of lenient bills proposed did not increase, and actually remained quite low. Finally, like in the House, when there is no major focusing event the number of restrictive bills being proposed reached their lowest, and in this case, the number of lenient bills proposed reached their highest. The data for the

Senate when it is controlled by the Democrats demonstrates: (1) that there is a slight impact in bill introduction in the Senate when there is a focusing event; (2) the number of restrictive bills proposed reaches its highest in post-focusing event Congresses events; and (3) the number of restrictive bills reaches its lowest when there are no major focusing events and the number of lenient bills reaches its highest.

The data for when Democrats control a chamber of Congress demonstrates that focusing events impact gun bill proposals in the House and the Senate. When there are major focusing events, lenient bill proponents tend to back down, but surprisingly, restrictive bill proponents do not appear to capitalize by quickly introducing large amounts of restrictive legislation. The true battleground, especially in the case of the House, appears to be in post-focusing event Congresses. The reason for this is due to the fact that restrictive bill proponents are given an entire new term to introduce legislation and lenient bill proponents have allowed for a cooling-off period. Lastly, when there are no major focusing events, restrictive bill proposals decline significantly. When there are no focusing events to draw attention, gun control policy is not a salient issue to restrictive bill proponents. However, when there are no major focusing events, lenient bill proponents use this as a time to propose the greatest amounts of lenient legislation. We now turn to a discussion of when the Republicans control Congress (see Figure 3.9).

The data above provides us with some surprising results. First, we find that when there is a major focusing event, the number of restrictive bills in the House when it is Republican controlled reaches its highest point and the number of lenient bills proposed reaches its lowest point. Second, we find that in post-focusing event Congresses the number of restrictive bills proposed drops considerably when compared to when there are major focusing events, and the number of lenient bills proposed increases. Third, the number of restrictive bills proposed when there are no major focusing events reaches its lowest point, but the number of lenient bills proposed stays the same.

The data on the House when it is Republican controlled has a few differences when compared to earlier trends. First, the largest number of restrictive bills being proposed occurs when there is a major focusing event, and not during post-focusing event Congresses. Second, there is never a major increase in lenient bill proposals. This is somewhat surprising. One could assume that when there are no major focusing events

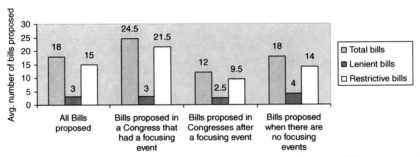

FIGURE 3.10 Average number of bills proposed when the Republicans control the Senate (1963–2008)

and the Republicans control the House there would be large number of lenient gun bills being proposed; however, this is not the case.

When we turn to examining the Senate data (see Figure 3.10), the trends that we find here are incongruent with trends seen in earlier figures. First, when there is a major focusing event, the number of restrictive Senate bills proposed increases to its highest point, which is not surprising; however, the number of lenient bills proposed does not change. Second, the lowest number of bills proposed occurs after post-focusing event Congresses. The number of total bills, the number of restrictive bills, and the number of lenient bills all reach their lowest point. Finally, when there are no major focusing events, lenient bill proposals reach their highest point, but the number of restrictive bills proposed is considerably higher than one might assume based on trends seen in previous figures.

The data on the Senate when it is Republican controlled shows some intriguing trends. First, the number of lenient bills proposed has very little variation and the numbers proposed are quite low, which is surprising. The second surprising trend is that during the normal battleground of bill proposals, post-focusing event Congresses, the number of all bill proposals are at their lowest.

The data for when the Congress is Republican controlled demonstrates that focusing events do appear to impact gun bill proposals. In both chambers of Congress, when there is a major focusing event there is an immediate outpouring of gun control bill proposals; however, in both chambers post-focusing event Congresses, have a smaller number of bills being proposed. Thus, when Republicans control Congress there may be an immediate agenda attention because of a focusing event, but after a cooling-off period the issue appears to become less salient. However, the most surprising aspect of the data is that the number of lenient bills being proposed in both chambers of Congress was not higher.

The discussion above provided us with insight on how Congress behaved when it was controlled by the two parties. The next section goes one step further and compares the relationship of the president with the Congress. There are eight figures in this section. Figures 3.11–3.14 compare gun bill proposals when there is a Democrat President with a Democrat House, Republican House, Democrat Senate, and a Republican Senate. Figures 3.15–3.18 compare gun bill proposals when there is a Republican President with a Republican House, Democrat House, Republican Senate, and a Democrat Senate.

Figure 3.11 demonstrates that when there is a major focusing event and the Democrats control both the Presidency and the House the number of restrictive bills being proposed is at its highest. The number of lenient bills proposed under these conditions is extremely low. The normal battleground for bill proposals is post-focusing event Congresses.

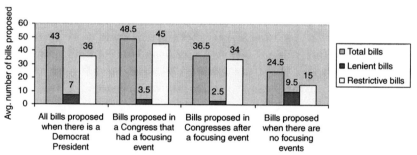

FIGURE 3.11 Average number of bills proposed when Democrats control the Presidency and the House (1963–2008)

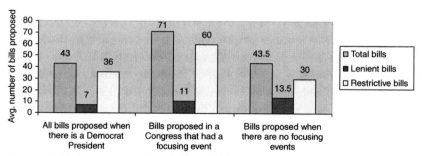

FIGURE 3.12 Average number of House bills proposed when Democrat President and Republican House (1963–2008)

However, in the case of the Democrats controlling both the House and the Presidency, the amount of lenient bills being proposed maintains a very low level. However, when there are no major focusing events, the number of restrictive gun control bills being proposed reaches its all-time low, and the number of lenient bills being proposed reaches its all-time high.

When we turn to a discussion of bill proposals when there is a Democrat President and a Republican House, we notice that the number of restrictive bills being proposed when there are major focusing events is high; we also notice that the number of lenient bills being proposed is considerably higher than the number of lenient bills being proposed when there is a Democrat House. When there are no major focusing events, the number of lenient bills being proposed reaches their highest point, and the number of restrictive bills being proposed reaches their lowest point.

When we compare the data, it appears that focusing events do lead to more gun bill proposals. The biggest difference is that when there is a Republican House as opposed to a Democrat House, the number of lenient bills being proposed is higher. However, interestingly, when there are no major focusing events there are actually more restrictive bills being proposed when there is a Republican House rather than when there is a Democrat House, but this may be a product of there being a low n. We now turn to examine the relationship between a Democrat President and the Senate.

When we look at the Senate data for when there is a Democrat President and the Senate is controlled by the Democrats, we find that the number of gun control bills proposed when there is a major focusing event is actually lower than the overall average for when there is a Democrat President. The number of bills proposed in post-focusing event Congresses was nearly identical to the overall average for when there is a Democrat President. Interestingly, when there are no major focusing events the number of gun control bills proposed in the Senate is extremely low. We find that the number of lenient bills being proposed under this condition is actually higher than the number of restrictive bills proposed. Thus, when we consider the data for Figure 3.13, we find that major focusing events appear to impact the number of gun control bills proposed in Senate when it is controlled by the Democrats and there is a Democrat President.

Figure 3.14 takes into account when there is a Democrat President and a Republican Senate. The data would lead us to believe that major

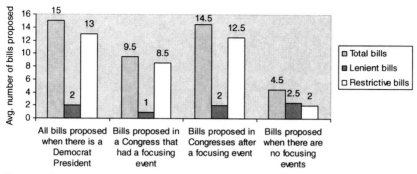

FIGURE 3.13 Average number of bills proposed when Democrats control the Presidency and the Senate (1963–2008)

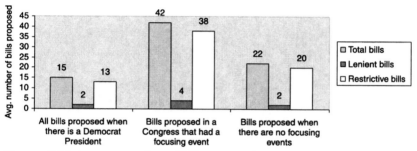

FIGURE 3.14 Average number of bills proposed when Democrat President and Republican Senate (1963–2008)

focusing events impact the number of bills proposed in the Senate when there is a Republican Senate and a Democrat President. However, the numbers in this section are extremely skewed because there was an *n* of only one, because of this very low *n*, it is hard for me to make many accurate predictions from the graph in Figure 3.14.

Figures 3.15–3.18 examine the relationship between a Republican President and the House and Senate: the first two examine this role with the House and the second two examine this role with the Senate.

Figure 3.15 examines when there is a Republican House and a Republican President. When there was a post-focusing event in Congress, the number of lenient bills proposed dropped slightly; however, the number of restrictive bills jumped considerably. When we examine the numbers for when there are no major focusing events, the number of lenient bills proposed stays at a near constant level, but the number of lenient bills drops significantly. The data suggests

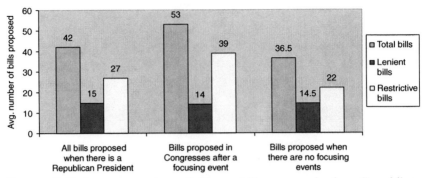

FIGURE 3.15 Average number of House bills proposed when Republican President and Republican House (1963–2008)

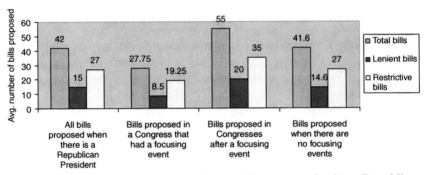

FIGURE 3.16 Average number of House bills proposed when Republican President and Democrat House (1963–2008)

that when there is a Republican President and a Republican House, major focusing events can and will lead to restrictive gun control bill proposals in the subsequent Congress; however, the number of lenient bills proposed does not appear to be impacted by whether an event is present or not.

Figure 3.16 examines when there is a Democrat House and a Republican President. We find that when there is a major focusing event, the number of lenient and restrictive House bills proposed were at their lowest. However, during post-focusing event Congresses, the number of both lenient and restrictive gun control bills proposed reached their highest levels. This trend has been seen throughout the data. Also, the number of bills proposed when there are no major focusing events is comparable to the overall average of bills proposed for when there is a Republican President. The data suggests that major focusing events impact gun bill

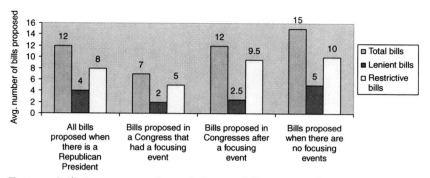

FIGURE 3.17 Average number of Senate bills proposed when Republican President and Republican Senate (1963–2008)

proposals; in particular, it appears that it impacts gun bill proposals during post-focusing event Congresses. Lastly, when we compare the data from Figures 3.15 and 3.16, it demonstrates that when there is a major focusing event and there is a Republican President, there will still be considerable levels of restrictive gun control legislation proposed after a major focusing event.

Figures 3.17 and 3.18 examine the influence of a Republican President on the Senate: the first examines the influence of a Republican President on a Republican Senate and the second chart examines the influence of a Republican President on a Democrat Senate.

Figure 3.17 demonstrates that when there is a Republican President and a Republican Senate, the number of bills proposed when there is a major focusing event is actually lower than the overall average number of Senate bills proposed when there is a Republican President. The number of restrictive and lenient bills proposed both decrease. When there is post-focusing event Congress, the number of bills proposed closely resembles the overall average when there is a Republican President. The biggest difference is that there are fewer lenient bills proposed, and higher restrictive bills proposed. Lastly, and oddly, the largest number of bills proposed is when there are no major focusing events. During this period of time there are more lenient and more restrictive bills proposed than at any other time. The trend seen in Figure 3.17 goes against the majority of the previous figures and the trends seen there.

Figure 3.18 demonstrates that when there is a Republican President and a Democrat Senate, the number of total bills proposed when there is a major focusing event declines, but there is actually more restrictive

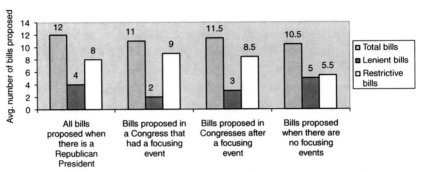

FIGURE 3.18 Average number of Senate bills proposed when Republican President and Democrat Senate (1963–2008)

bills proposed than the overall average for when there is a Republican President. When there is post-focusing event Congress, the number of bills proposed closely resembles average for Senate bill proposals when there is a Republican President. The biggest discrepancy once again comes from less lenient bills and more restrictive bills. Finally, when we look at the bills proposed when there are no major focusing events, we see that the number of restrictive bills proposed is at its lowest and the number of lenient bills proposed is at its highest. The trends seen in the graph in Figure 3.18 closely resemble the trends seen in earlier figures.

Overall, when we consider all of the figures, the data indicates a number of things. First, when there is a major focusing event, the Congress that contains the event generally sees a significant drop in lenient bill proposals, but not a large increase in restrictive bill proposals. Second, when there is a post-focusing event Congress, the number of restrictive and lenient bills proposed tends to increase significantly. This suggests that after there has been a cooling-off period lenient bill proponents attempt to counter restrictive legislation, and restrictive bill proponents propose a plethora of new restrictive bill proposals. Finally, the data indicates that when there are no major focusing events, generally speaking, the number of restrictive bills proposed is at their lowest and the number of lenient bills proposed is at their highest. Thus, when there are no major focusing events to drive attention, restrictive bill proponents do not attempt to drive through as much new restrictive legislation; however, lenient bill proponents use this time to try and remove or change existing restrictive legislation.

Does Agenda Attention Result in
Formulation? Not Necessarily

The discussion above demonstrated that when there is a major focusing event, agenda attention to gun control policy increased, in particular, to restrictive gun control bill proposals. The data also demonstrated that in post-focusing event Congresses, agenda attention to both restrictive and lenient bills increased significantly. Lastly, when there were no major focusing events, restrictive agenda attention generally reached its lowest point; whereas, lenient agenda attention was often at its highest.

When discussing major themes of the book in Chapter 2, I stated that focusing events may lead to increased agenda attention, but they would never lead to new gun control bills being formulated when there was unified Republican control, or divided government. I also theorized that when there was unified Democrat control of government focusing events would rarely lead to new gun control policy; however, I didn't believe that this policy would be significant and comprehensive in nature rather it would be incremental changes.

Since 1963, 687 restrictive House bills have been proposed and 234 restrictive Senate bills. In that same time period, there have been 275 lenient House bills proposed and 71 lenient Senate bills. Of these, only six major pieces of federal firearm legislation have been created. Three of these were restrictive bills and three were lenient.

Table 3.9 examines the six pieces of federal gun control legislation that have been crafted since 1963. The data demonstrates that for every piece of lenient legislation that has been created, there was a Republican President and a Republican Senate, in one instance, the 1986 Gun Owners Protection Act, there was a Democrat House along with the Republican President and the Republican Senate. For every piece of restrictive legislation that has been created there was a Democrat President, a Democrat House, and a Democrat Senate.

The figures in this chapter focused on gun bill proposals and when they were proposed. Figure 3.17 demonstrates that lenient federal gun control bills have been formulated when there were no major focusing events, and there was Republican control of at least the Presidency and one chamber of Congress.

On the flip side, the three pieces of restrictive federal legislation that were created tended to coincide with major focusing events or followed post-focusing event Congresses. The Gun Control Act of 1968 was created immediately after two major focusing events. The Brady Bill and the

Table 3.9 Formulated and implemented gun control laws 1963–2008

Congress	Bill	Type	President	House	Senate	Was there a focusing event?
90	1968 Gun Control Act	Restrictive	Democrat	Democrat	Democrat	2 focusing events
99	Gun Owners Protection Act	Lenient	Republican	Democrat	Republican	No events
103	Assault Weapons Ban	Restrictive	Democrat	Democrat	Democrat	Followed Congress that had event
103	Brady Bill	Restrictive	Democrat	Democrat	Democrat	Followed Congress that had event
109	Bill to prevent seizure of weapons during crisis	Lenient	Republican	Republican	Republican	No events
109	Bill to protect gun manufacturers from being liable	Lenient	Republican	Republican	Republican	No events

Assaults Weapon Ban were created during the 103rd Congress, which was a post-focusing event Congress.

Focusing events tend to draw increased attention to the gun control issue, no matter which party is in power. The data in the previous sections even demonstrated that more restrictive bills were proposed in some situations when there was Republican control rather than Democrat control; however, even with the increase in agenda attention there have only been three pieces of restrictive federal gun control legislation to be created over the course of my study and none of them were created when there was Republican control of the Presidency or either branch of the Congress.

Focusing events draw increased attention to the gun control issue when there is Democrat control, in particular, to the number of restrictive bill proposed during the Congress that contained the major focusing event and post-focusing event Congresses. However, of the hundreds of bills that have been proposed when there were major focusing events, or was a post-focusing event Congress, only three pieces of restrictive gun control legislation were created. All three pieces of legislation were relatively modest in their goals. This suggests that even when there is Democrat control of the Presidency and/or the Congress it is exceedingly difficult for restrictive gun control proponents to drive through policy even when there is heightened agenda attention due to a major focusing event.

In the first portion of this chapter we discussed the significance of public attitudes on gun control policy and found that it had very little impact on the creation of federal gun control laws. This portion of Chapter 3 demonstrated the significance of political parties and government structure in the determination of gun control policy outcomes.

When we consider government structure, it is obvious that the presidential democracy of the United States was not designed to be efficient in nature. There were literally hundreds of restrictive and lenient gun control bills proposed in the United States during the period of my study, yet only six became law. This suggests that for a bill to become law it needs significant support within both branches of Congress and the president. Thus, government structure is very important in determining the outcome of gun control bills in the United States; however, it is not the only significant factor.

The second very important factor is the role of political parties. The Republicans have a long-standing tradition of favoring lenient gun control laws. The gun control bills that were created during their control of national government have followed this tradition. Likewise, the

Democrats have more of a tradition of wanting to limit firearms. And when there has been unified control of national government by the Democrats we have seen the only pieces of restrictive gun control policy created. Thus, the party in power and its political leanings and affiliations are very important in determining whether a gun violence focusing event will go past the agenda-setting stage and on to formulation and implementation.

Thus far in this chapter, we have determined that public opinion is not nearly as important in influencing gun control policy as the government structure and the political parties of the United States. The last portion of this chapter goes into a rich analysis of another very important factor: interest group pressures.

Thus far it has been difficult to provide a direct link to NRA's involvement in influencing gun bill proposals; however, to disregard the significance of its power in swaying policy makers would be naïve. The Republican Party, which has strong support for the NRA among its ranks, is significantly influenced by the NRA's lobbying efforts. The NRA has also been very influential when it has directed its efforts at Democrat Congressional members who come from districts that have populations that favor more lenient gun control measures. In this last portion of Chapter 3, I provide more evidence of a linkage of NRA power to the prevention of new gun control laws after a major gun violence event by using the *New York Times* to create a narrative of these events and their subsequent outcomes.

The *New York Times* Coverage of Major Focusing Events and Gun Control Policy 1963–2008

The final section of Chapter 3 examines the major gun violence focusing events that have occurred over the past half century. There have been many shootings and slayings in that time frame; thus it was difficult to identify the key events that could be characterized as a major focusing event, and what events would be considered less important on the national level. The major focusing events that were identified and used in the preceding section were also used in this section.

Sadly, slayings that only involve two or three people are often not even discussed by the *New York Times*, unless the murders were in the New York metropolitan area. What gun violence events that truly drew the attention of the *New York Times* for an extended period of time were not these less sensational slayings, but the truly shocking and horrendous events. Mass murders of a large number of people by a firearm drew major attention from both the public and the *New York Times*. The mass murder events that were identified were the Purdy Massacre in Stockton, California; the Killeen, Texas Massacre; the Columbine slayings; and the Virginia Tech murders. I realize that there have been other slayings where a number of people were killed; however, those events did not draw the same level of attention as these.

The other types of major gun violence focusing event that drew the publics and media's attention were assassinations or the attempted assassinations of major political figures: the assassination of John F. Kennedy; the assassination of Martin Luther King Jr; the assassination of Robert Kennedy; and the attempted assassination of Ronald Reagan. Though assassinations are different than the wanton killings of a mass murder, they both draw attention to the gun control policy alternatives. Both types of events tend to lead to gun control bill proponents to introduce new restrictive legislation. (It will be noted that other assassination attempts were excluded from this discussion. Like some mass murders, I found these events to have less national bearing on potential gun control than the ones used in this analysis.)

This section does a case-by-case narrative of the major focusing events mentioned above to discuss the public, the media, politicians, and interest group views on the event and what should be done to prevent such events from occurring again in the future. I also discuss the major pieces of legislation that were created and how effective policy makers and interest groups believed the legislation would be.

The 1960s: The John F. Kennedy, Martin Luther King Jr, and Robert Kennedy Assassinations, and the Birth of Gun Control Act of 1968

The first major focusing event that occurred in my study was the assassination of John F. Kennedy on November 22, 1963. After the Kennedy assassination literally hundreds of articles were written that discussed the assassination. However, only a few discussed the political implications of the event.

There were large numbers of foreign firearms being imported into the United States at the time of the Kennedy assassination, such as the Italian made rifle that was used for the assassination, and there

was a bill introduced to curb these imports. The bill had been introduced in August of 1963, but it was expected that the event would lead
to an increased desire by lawmakers to see this legislation was created
(Godbout, November 25, 1963).

Many gun enthusiasts and gun owners feared that the assassination of
the president would lead to new restrictive laws that would take firearms
away from them. NRA Vice President Franklin L. Orth, wrote to the *New
York Times* to explain the NRA's view on potential new gun control legislation. Orth argued that the NRA's primary goal was to teach and train
people on how properly to use firearms. Orth stated that "the right to
keep and bear arms is not obsolete, as has been suggested. Without this
right and all of its ramifications, this country could be unalterably weakened in its defense posture." Interestingly, Orth argued that gun control
laws in the United States would make the country look weak to potential
invaders and enemies (Orth, December 3, 1963).

The next two focusing events took place in 1968. These two infamous
events were the assassination of Martin Luther King Jr and the assassination of Robert Kennedy. The assassination of Martin Luther King Jr
on April 4, 1968 drew massive amounts of attention from the *New York
Times*. On April 12, 1968, Harold Glassen of the Michigan branch of
the NRA stated that the "assassination of Martin Luther King Jr was a
senseless, cruel murder." He went on further to state that "every time a
prominent person is shot it does create an emotional atmosphere which
has its effect but it should have no effect on gun control legislation"
(Associated Press, April 12, 1968).

One of the primary proponents for gun control legislation was
Senator Dodd, Democrat of Connecticut. Senator Dodd proposed a bill
that would provide more restrictions on mail order firearms and restrictions on handguns. The bill was successfully pushed through the House
Judiciary Committee on April 7, three days after the assassination of
King. The Dodd bill was added to President Johnson's proposed Crime
Bill. It, along with the Crime Bill, would lead to the Firearms Act of
1968. The lobbying efforts of the NRA had made it very difficult for the
Dodd bill to gain much support. However, due to the politically charged
atmosphere caused by the assassination of Martin Luther King Jr, the
time was right for the creation of new gun control legislation (Franklin,
April 21, 1968).

The Dodd bill was just the tip of the iceberg in the reaction to the
King assassination. On April 28, Dr Thomas Pettigrew, a renowned social
psychologist, wrote the *New York Times* calling for increased gun control

legislation because of our society being violent by structure, not by nature. In this article he argued that the NRA influence was preventing Congress from doing the right thing and creating gun control legislation up to what he termed "a level with more urban societies." He said that these laws needed to be updated to protect both the common citizen and our country's leaders (Pettigrew, April 28, 1968).

On May 10, 1968, President Johnson appealed to the Senate for stricter gun control laws. The president was quoted as saying: "What in the name of conscience will it take to pass a truly effective gun control law. Has not the high-powered mail order rifle brought tragedy enough to America?" Johnson urged that the bill needed to be passed rapidly because "the mugger and murderer will not wait—neither must we" (Associated Press, May 10, 1968). On May 15, 1968 Senator Edward Kennedy of Massachusetts was quoted in the *New York Times* as having serious problems with the weakness of the gun control provisions in the Senates crime bill and sought further restrictive provisions to be added. He was quoted as saying: "It amazes me that we continue to tolerate a system of laws which makes it so outrageously easy for any criminal, insane person, drug addict, or child to obtain lethal firearms which can be used to rain violence and death on innocent people" (*New York Times*, May 15, 1968).

On May 17, certain provisions were added to the Senate crime control bill. If the bill were implemented, it would ban the importation of surplus handguns and military weapons, along with preventing the sale of firearms to criminals. The Senate did eliminate the proposed provision of banning the mail order of rifles and shotguns. Senator Edward Kennedy of Massachusetts proposed an amendment to ban mail order firearms to the Dodd bill, the gun control provisions of the Senate crime bill, but his amendment was voted down. President Johnson expressed extreme disappointment that this provision was dropped and Senator Dodd was quoted as saying: "How many Presidents have to be assassinated, how many Dr. Martin Luther Kings have to be killed before we come to our senses?" However, the leading opposition in the Senate, Republican Senator Roman L. Hruska of Nebraska, argued that only about 500 murders a year result from the use of rifles and shotguns and that the nation's 20 million hunters should not be penalized by restrictions on their sale (Finney, May 17, 1968).

In the waning hours of June 5, 1968 presidential candidate Robert Kennedy was assassinated. The following day, June 6, 1968, the House moved quickly in passing broad anticrime legislation, including the interstate sales of handguns and surplus military weapons (though controls on rifles and shotguns were still absent). It was believed that the House crime bill would not have included any provisions to include gun control restrictions; however, the assassination of Robert Kennedy was the final confirmation that legislation needed to be created to curb violence. Even House Republican Leader Gerald R. Ford stated: "Surely there can be no further quibbling about the urgent need for tougher law enforcement legislation" (Finney, June 6, 1968).

Also on June 6, Franklin Orth, executive vice president of the NRA commented on the assassination of Robert Kennedy: "This is a terrible tragedy, a senseless act." But when asked would stricter gun control legislation have prevented the act he stated: "I honestly believe it would not have prevented this crime. I know of no law in existence or proposed that could have prevented it" (Associated Press, June 6, 1968). The National leader for the NRA, Harold W. Glassen, also expressed disdain for the creation of any new gun control laws. He was quoted as saying: "The simple fact is there is no gun control law that the mind of man could conceive that would have had the slightest effect in preventing any of the assassinations of our day." He also stated that "let's not punish 40 million American Sportsmen because of the fact that there are some kooks in American today." He did state that the NRA supported the legislation barring the sale of guns to juveniles, delinquents, to drug addicts, and to convicts. He also stated the NRA supported waiting periods, but did not support the registration of every gun in America because it would be too complex to carry out (Grose, June 8, 1968).

On June 7, 1968, President Johnson reacted to the death of Senator Robert F. Kennedy by imploring the Congress to create stricter gun control legislation. President Johnson stated in private and public discussions that he wanted to capitalize on the shock of the Kennedy shooting to bring the sale of rifles and shotgun under tight control. The bill that was created by the House and passed overwhelmingly was still considered to be too weak by President Johnson, and he stated that he had several more restrictive measures that needed to become law. The stricter provisions that Johnson wanted to add to the bill were: the prohibition of the sale of rifles and shotguns by mail and in any manner to persons under the age of 18, prohibition of the sale firearms to residents of another state; the provisions also would prohibit the criminal and the insane from being able to purchase firearms.

In discussing the bill, President Johnson stated: "It leaves the deadly commerce in lethal shotguns and rifles without effective control-55 long months after the mail order murder of President John F. Kennedy. So today, I call upon the Congress in the name of sanity, and in the name of an aroused nation, to give American the gun control law it needs." Johnson also showed aggravation with Congress and its deference to the NRA. Johnson was quoted as saying: "The voices of the few must no longer prevail over the interests of the many" (Frankel, June 7, 1968).

On June 8, 1968, Democrat Senate leader Mike Mansfield argued that even with the pressure of the White House to add the more restrictive gun control provisions of President Johnson, he doubted that they would be adopted. He also suggested that the NRA was not nearly as powerful or influential as the White House made it to be (Finney, June 8, 1968). However, Senator Millard Tydings, a Democrat from Maryland, accused the NRA of being nothing more than a front for gun makers whose lobbying power scares Congress away from strong gun control legislation. Senator Tydings also vowed to introduce legislation to require the registration and licensing of every privately owned firearm (Associated Press, June 9, 1968).

On June 10, Senator Dodd proposed new legislation that would ban the interstate shipment of mail order rifles and shotguns. The bill also proposed the registration of all firearms and the prohibition of anyone being able to purchase ammunition unless they could prove their weapon was registered (*New York Times*, June 11, 1968). However, Republican leader of the Senate Everett McKinley of Illinois stated that "There is enough gun legislation on the books now." And Democratic leader Mike Mansfield of Montana stated that "no matter how stringent new laws might be, none represented a cure-all." The two leaders agreed that new gun control legislation did not need to be created at the time (Finney, June 11, 1968).

On June 11, 1968, the House version of the Dodd bill was blocked by a 16–16 vote in the House Judiciary Committee. President Johnson was not impressed by this course of events. He stated that: "It was a bitter disappointment to all Americans and to the President." He also hoped that "the House Judiciary Committee will promptly reconsider this shocking blow to the safety of every citizen in this country" (Finney, June 11, 1968).

After Johnson's disapproval of how gun control legislation was being discarded, there was a large outpouring of public outrage that no gun control legislation was created. Senators who had been opposed to new gun control legislation stated that they would now favor the new provisions and would likely vote for President Johnson's provisions (Finney, June 12, 1968).

On June 14, the NRA notified its members that "the right of sportsmen to obtain, own and use firearms for proper lawful purposes is in the greatest jeopardy in the history of our country . . . Unless the sportsmen of America clearly express their views without delay to their Senators and Congressmen, individuals will be prohibited from acquiring long guns in interstate commerce and general firearms registration will become a reality." Senator Tydings accused the NRA of "creating a campaign of calculated hysteria and distortion to defeat reasonable gun control legislation" (Finney, June 15, 1968).

On June 24, 1968 President Johnson called for the registering of all firearms and the licensing of all firearms owners. Johnson said that he did not want the new bill to slow down the proposed amendments to the anticrime bill that would ban the interstate shipment of shotguns and rifles by mail (Frankel, June 25, 1968).

Between early July and early September there was a lull on the new restrictive gun control measures. The bill and its provisions were initially supported, but delaying tactics by opponents led to several months of standstill. On September 11, 1968 Attorney General Ramsey Clark asked the Senate to include the registration and licensing of all firearms. However support for a system where there would be blanket registration was not widely supported in the Senate (Finney, September 10, 1968).

On September 18, the Senate passed a gun control bill restricting the interstate sale of rifles and shotguns. However, the proposal for blanket registration and licensing failed to be added to the bill, that proposal was defeated by a 55–31 vote (Finney, September 18, 1968).

On October 22, President Johnson signed what would be the final version of the gun bill that would be included in the 1968 Omnibus Crime Bill, and what would be widely known as the Gun Control Act of 1968. Johnson was pleased with the restrictions on the interstate shipment of rifles and shotguns; however, he was displeased that a blanket registration and licensing system was not implemented. He argued that the NRA was responsible when he stated that: "The voices that blocked these safeguards were not the voices of an aroused nation. They were the voices of a powerful gun lobby that has prevailed for the moment in an election year" (Hunter, October 23, 1968).

The assassination of President Kennedy in 1963 and the assassinations of Martin Luther King Jr and Robert Kennedy in 1968 led to a vigorous debate for the creation of new gun control. However, as has been demonstrated in the previous discussion, the power of the NRA was evident in preventing various provisions from being added to the 1968 Gun

Control Act. The NRA actively sought aid from its members, and gun control proponents actively blamed the NRA for the failure of their gun control laws from seeing the light of day. The Gun Control Act of 1968 that emerged from the political maelstrom was far weaker than gun control proponents had sought.

The assassinations of the 1960s brought significant attention to the gun control debate. Gun controls of various types were introduced at the federal level after each of the focusing events discussed in this section; however, only one federal law was created and it was widely considered by gun control proponents to be too weak. Thus, major gun violence focusing events did lead to increased agenda attention yet their impact in creating significant federal laws was minimal and hard-won.

The Early and Mid-1980s: The Attempted Assassination of Ronald Reagan; the Gun Owners Protection Act

On March 31, 1981, President Reagan was nearly killed in an attempted assassination. The shock of this event was felt immediately across the country and by policy makers. Members of the Senate reacted immediately to the event. Senator Edward Kennedy, Democrat from Massachusetts, stated: "All of us who care about this country and who care about our fellow citizens bear an important responsibility in whatever way we possibly can to rid this society and to rid this country of the kind of violence and hatred that we have seen." And Senator Daniel Patrick Moynihan, Democrat from New York, stated: "How much shooting is going to have to happen before we get rid of those guns?" (Tolchin, March 31, 1981).

Gun control proponents immediately attempted a push for more gun control laws on pistols in the wake of the president's shooting. Nelson T. Shields, Chairman of Handgun Control, Inc. stated that public pressure for such legislation (restrictive gun control laws) had been mounting. Gun control proponents felt that new laws needed to be created because the enforcement provisions of the 1968 Gun Control Act had been weakened, and it was thus a failure. However, John M. Snyder, a chief lobbyist for gun groups, predicted that the rush of activity (the surge on gun control agenda attention) would be nothing more than that, after the excitement was over, Congress, if anything, would be more likely to pass a bill sponsored by the NRA to weaken the enforcement power of the government. Snyder reasoned that this was the case because of the strong sentiment against gun control by members of Congress and the president. Snyder called Reagan the "most pro-gun President we have had in many years" (*New York Times*, March 31, 1981).

On April 1, 1981, new restrictive gun control legislation was urged by some in Congress; however, there was little hope by most Congressional members that new legislation would be brought forth due to the shooting. Speaker of the House Thomas P. O'Neil Jr, Democrat from Massachusetts, stated: "I doubt that a general gun control bill would meet with very much success around here. Personally, I'm for gun control, but realistically I don't think it can pass." Senator Dodd, who had pushed vigorously for the gun control that was created in 1968, stated: "The National Rifle Association is the most effective lobby in Washington. There will be a lot of rhetoric and a lot of talk, but I don't see anything happening, unfortunately." Other Democrats stated that even bringing up the idea of gun control was "devastatingly counterproductive" for liberals because it provided a rallying cry for conservative Republicans (Roberts, April 1, 1981).

On April 2, 1981, Senator Edward Kennedy proposed new gun control legislation in the Senate. Kennedy sought to compromise on gun control legislation and proposed more moderate controls, and not the broad sweeping legislation that he had proposed in the past. However, other Senators were skeptical that the legislation would come to pass. Senator Howard M. Metzenbaum, Democrat of Ohio, stated: "I would not be very optimistic that any gun control legislation would move very rapidly." Senator James A. McClure, Republican of Idaho, who was a leading foe of gun control stated: "the proposals of Kennedy were more cosmetic than real." He also went on to say about the proposed legislation to limit cheap firearms: "A large percentage of cheap handguns are in the homes of people who want to defend themselves because the criminal justice system doesn't" (Roberts, April 2, 1981).

On April 4, 1981, Senator Kennedy, in discussing his proposal to restrict pistols, stated "(Gun control) is not an easy issue for any officeholder or candidate." General sentiment on Capitol Hill was that Kennedy's statement was an understatement. Congressional members have stated that supporting tighter gun laws has been one of the most frustrating and fruitless of legislative tasks in recent years. The reason for this failing most law makers agreed could be directly attributed to the NRA. Representative Jim Wright, Democrat from Texas stated: "Every member of Congress tells the same story. There are hundreds of people, in some cases literally thousands, who never write to them on any other subject, but become irate and paranoid and very frightened at any suggestion of gun control" (Roberts, April 5, 1981).

On June 16, 1981, President Reagan himself voiced his opinion on the gun control issue. President Reagan favored gun control legislation, but the type of legislation he favored did not sit well with many gun control proponents. Reagan advocated that stricter penalties should be provided for people who use firearms in the commission of a crime, like the laws he had signed in California. Reagan believed that gun control laws "were virtually unenforceable" and did not favor the restrictions proposed by Senator Kennedy (King, June 17, 1981).

Reagan's failure to support restrictive gun control measures led to the demise of the gun control proposals of Senator Kennedy. The next piece of major gun control legislation to be created was not restrictive in nature; rather it was a major piece of lenient gun control law that effectively destroyed the 1968 Gun Control Act. The next portion of this discussion goes into a brief description of attitudes of policy makers during the creation of the Gun Owners Protection Act of 1986.

The 1986 Gun Owners Protection Act did not come into being without opposition. The NRA, which had long worked with police groups, created a rift with many police organizations by attempting to force through the law that would loosen gun control restrictions. A group of 12 national police organizations met to denounce the proposed bill (Burnham, January 31, 1986).

On April 10, 1986, the House of Representatives approved a bill making it easier to buy, sell, and transport firearms across state lines. The primary aim of the new legislation, which was sanctioned and driven by the NRA, was to allow for easier interstate movement of firearms. The easing of the laws demonstrated that the NRA's lobbying prowess was powerful as ever (Greenhouse, April 11, 1986).

On May 19, 1986, the Gun Owners Protection Act was signed into law by President Reagan. The president stated that he was happy with the law because it "protected law-abiding citizens without diminishing the effectiveness of criminal law enforcement" (Associated Press, May 20, 1986).

The Gun Owners Protection Act became law when there had been no major focusing events for several years. The bill is a testament to the power of the NRA's power in lobbying to create new lenient gun control laws. The next portion of this section goes into a discussion of two major focusing, the Purdy Massacre and the Killeen, Texas Massacre, and their impact on gun control legislation in the early 1990s.

The Late 1980s and Early 1990s: The Purdy Massacre, the Killeen, Texas Massacre, the Brady Bill, and the Assault Weapons Ban

On January 17, 1989, Patrick Edward Purdy used an AK-47 machine gun to kill 5 children and wound 29 others and teacher. On January 28, 1989, a bill was introduced in the US Congress to ban the sale of military assault weapons to the public. The bill was introduced as a direct response to the Purdy Massacre (Reinhold, January 28, 1989).

The NRA was not impressed by the proposed ban. David W. Conover, a lobbyist for the NRA, stated: "It's called an assault weapon by people who want to ban it, a rifle by those who don't. It has a romantic sound to it. But there's no difference between semiautomatic rifles that are assault and those that are conventional." Another NRA lobbyist, John Snyder, stated that the reason the federal government wanted to ban assault rifles was because: "When the criminal justice system is embarrassed, it tries to blame somebody else, in this case gun owners" (Reinhold, January 28, 1989).

On February 16, 1989, President Bush made his stance on the proposed new gun controls known. President Bush stated: "If you are suggesting that every pistol or rifle should be banned, I would strongly oppose that. I would strongly go after the criminals who use these guns. But, I'm not about to suggest that a semi-automated hunting rifle be banned. Absolutely not. Am I opposed to AK-47's fully automated? Am I in favor of supporting the law that says they shouldn't come in here? Yes" (Boyd, February 17, 1989).

However, on March 17, 1989, President Bush made a new statement on the gun control debate. In a month's time he had softened his view on more restrictive gun control measures and said that an accommodation needed to be made. He said his change in attitude was due to the high levels of public outcry and the concerns of police officers (Weinraub, March 18, 1989).

The NRA felt the pressure of both the public and lawmakers from the Purdy Massacre. In an interview, Wayne LaPierre, the executive director of the NRA's lobbying division, stated the views of the NRA on the proposed assault weapons ban. LaPierre stated: "The hysteria (the public outcry from the Purdy Massacre) on this is just unbelievable right now. Whenever you put an emotional label to an issue, it takes a while to get the truth out. What was needed on this issue was a cooling-off period to get the debate back in the real world and look at it gun by gun" (Dowd, March 18, 1989).

By mid-April, the discussion of the proposed Assault Weapons Ban had petered out. There was still intermittent mention of the bill in the *New York Times*, but for the most part they were editorial pieces asking where the president stood on the gun control issue, and the confusion of lawmakers on whether they should pursue the bill if the president was not fully behind it. Thus, the Purdy Massacre led to the Assault Weapons Ban first being mentioned by gun control advocates, but because of NRA pressures and reluctance by the Republican President Bush, the Assault Weapons Ban was placed on hold for several years.

On October 16, 1991, the Killen Texas Massacre, also known as the Luby's Massacre, took place. George Jo Hennard shot and killed 23 people. On October 17, 1991, the House overwhelmingly rejected a ban on the sale and ownership of semiautomatic weapons and multiple bullet gun clips. The vote stirred extreme controversy. Representative Chet Edwards, a freshman Democrat from the Texas district that contained Killeen, stated he had switched his opinion on gun control. He stated: "Don't let the tragedy in my district yesterday be the tragedy in your neighborhoods tomorrow. We cannot bring back the lives of 22 citizens lost yesterday. But with your vote we can save some lives." However, Representative Harold L. Volkmer, a Democrat from Missouri and strong opponent to gun control, stated: "It was not the pistol that caused those deaths." Gun control proponents were stunned by the vote. A chief lobbyist for gun control proponents, Jeffery Y. Muchnick stated: "This vote is disgraceful. It's hard to believe members are so callous when people are being killed in the streets" (Kraus, October 18, 1991).

The Killeen Texas Massacre was the worst mass murder in US history up until the Virginia Tech shooting. However, even with the event fresh in the minds of Congressional members, the House bill that was voted on two days after the shooting was overwhelmingly voted down. However, the Purdy Massacre and the Killeen Texas Massacre had a lingering impact on future gun control proposals. When President Clinton and the Democrats took control of the Presidency and both chambers of Congress in 1993, the impact of these focusing events once again came to the fore.

In early 1993, the battle for the Brady Bill, and, to a lesser extent, the Assault Weapons Ban began in earnest. In early August 1993, President Clinton declared his support for the Brady Bill. The Brady Bill's two main provisions at this time were a waiting period and a background check on all potential buyers of handguns (Eckholm, August 15, 1993).

On November 10, 1993 the House approved legislation that would require a buyer of a handgun to wait five business days before taking possession of it, but only after adding an amendment that would end the requirement after five years. This was the second time the bill had been passed in the House; the previous version of the bill had been killed in the Senate. Chair of the House Judiciary Committee, Jack Brooks, Democrat Texas, said that the bill "infringes on the rights of law abiding citizens" (Krauss, November 11, 1993).

On November 24, 1993, the Senate passed the Brady Bill. Sarah Brady, the wife of Reagan Press Secretary James Brady who was wounded in the attempted Reagan assassination, was the leading proponent of the bill. The NRA had lobbied against the bill vigorously but in the end failed to prevent its passage. Wayne LaPierre called the waiting period "unfair to honest, law abiding people. The criminals won't wait." However, major gun control proponents were ecstatic. Charles Schumer, Democrat Representative from New York, stated: "This is the first time since 1968 that the NRA has been beaten on a major issue, but it won't be the last. Lawmakers will learn that there is life after voting against the NRA." The victory of the Brady Bill heartened gun control proponents to attempt to create even more restrictive legislation, and thus a stronger push for the Assault Weapons Ban began (Krauss, November 25, 1993).

On May 1, 1994 the debate over an Assault Weapons Ban began in earnest. NRA spokesman Wayne LaPierre stated: "The good guns they don't want to ban and the guns they want to ban all fire the same. None fire any faster. None make any bigger holes. None shoot any harder. None make any bigger noise." The guns that LaPierre was referring to was 19 specific assault guns and copycat models and would also limit detachable magazines to 10 rounds (Associated Press, May 2, 1994).

In early May, the Assault Weapons Ban once again looked like it was doomed to failure. Charles Schumer, Democrat Representative from New York, stated that gun control proponents were still about 15 votes short for passage of the ban. NRA spokesman Wayne LaPierre stated: "I don't think you will see a big swing on this issue. People have staked out positions during their campaigns; they have staked them out for years. It is hard for us to win converts from their side; it's tough for them to win converts from our side" (Seelye, May 4, 1993). However, by May 9, enough Republicans had gone over to the gun control proponent side for the ban to be passed in the House. On August 25 the Senate also passed the Assault Weapons Ban.

Through the creation of the Brady Bill, the shootings of President Reagan and James Brady were constantly mentioned as a driving factor that initiated the bill. The Assault Weapons Ban was first proposed after the Purdy Massacre and even more public support for it was created after the Killeen Texas Massacre. Once there was a change in the Presidency, the door was opened for both bills to become law. It is evident that gun violence focusing events laid the initial groundwork for these two policies to be created; however, I still argue that the bills that were created were incremental in nature because of their limited overall impact. The Brady bill only added a few new provisions and the Assault Weapons Ban focused on only 19 weapons. Both the Brady Bill and the Assault Weapons Ban had amendments added that effectively killed them after a number of years. The Brady Bill had a provision in it that made five-day waiting periods expire after five years, and the Assault Weapons Ban expired in its entirety after ten years. These added provisions and amendments would not have been placed there had the NRA and its Republican allies not battled each bill every step of the way. At present, both the Assault Weapons Ban is defunct, and portions of the Brady Bill were deemed unconstitutional.

The Late 1990s to 2008: Columbine Slayings, Republican and NRA Victories of the 109th Congress, Virginia Tech Massacre

On April 20, 1999 two high school gun men shot and killed many of their fellow class mates in the worst high school shooting to have ever taken place. On the same day President Clinton remarked that he was "profoundly shocked and saddened" by the school shooting in Colorado, and he expressed the hope that the country would somehow find ways to prevent future bloodshed (Stout, April 21, 1999).

On April 26, an article discussing the NRA's tactics after gun violence focusing events illuminated some interesting facts. Gary Kleck, professor of criminology at Florida State, stated that the NRA typically draws back from the gun debate after a major violent crime. A memorandum that was being circulated by gun groups stated: "At this time I do not feel that a statement for widespread distribution to the media is appropriate because it has not been suggested and barring irresponsible exploitation by anti-gun groups, I do not believe that it will be suggested that fire-arms, or the promotion of the recreational use of firearms, are in anyway responsible for this tragedy" (Meier, April 26, 1999). This resembles the data from the previous section where lenient gun control bills dipped significant during Congressional terms where there were major focusing events.

Also on April 26, President Clinton planned to announce new gun pro-posals. The NRA was assigned blame for the shooting by the administra-tion indirectly. President Clinton's spokesman stated: "It's premature to assign blame. I think there is a consensus in this country that we need to do more. The president will propose doing more. And it's time for the NRA to get out of the past and get on the right side of this issue." However, many were not optimistic about gun control legislation being created because of the negative view on it from the Congress. The reason for this negative view by Congressional members stemmed back to the Assault Weapons Ban in 1994. President Clinton stated: "The fight for the Assault Weapons Ban cost 20 members their seats in Congress. The NRA is the reason the Republicans control the House." Senator Tom Daschle, Democrat South Dakota, stated: "I'm not sure that gun legislation is what we need." Rather he cited the internet and the media as being the prime suspect for the school shooting at Columbine (Seelye, April 27, 1999).

The question of whether the NRA had that severe of an impact on Congressional members has been debated. Robert Dreyfuss, in his study of the NRA and its political activities after the passage of the Brady Bill and the Assault Weapons Ban, makes some interesting conclusions. First, Dreyfuss found that the NRA was the nation's biggest spender on elec-tions in 1994. Second, the NRA targeted Democrats who had voted for gun control legislation and were not in safe seats. The NRA did not nec-essarily attack these legislators just on the gun control issue, but on a vari-ety of issues. The NRA would find what topics a Democrat Congressional member was weak on with their constituents, and would run attack ads in their districts based on these issues. Thus, the NRA showed a variety of tactics in eliminating competitors. The reason the NRA was able to spend so much money on elections in 1994 was because of its large support base and because of large donations from the gun industry (Dreyfuss 1995). Thus, the perception by Democrats that the NRA was one of the primary reasons that many of them were defeated in the 1994 election turns out to not only be a perception but a reality.

On May 6, 1999 new gun control measures were offered in the Senate. Citing the Columbine shooting specifically, Senator Charles E. Schumer,

Democrat from New York, stated that eight new gun bill provisions would be introduced. Schumer stated that he thought the new amendments to the bill would "maximize its impact on criminals and children while minimizing its impact on law abiding citizens." Trent Lott, Republican from Mississippi, in responding to the new gun bill proposals, stated: "I'm not sure if the solution to the prevention of this sort of problem like we had in Colorado is necessarily more federal legislation" (Bruni, May 7, 1999).

Support for the gun measures in the Senate continued, with some Republicans even switching sides on the debate. The proposed gun control amendments mostly were aimed at making it more difficult for children to obtain firearms; however, there were certain provisions that were included that would have led to new gun controls, which led to problems for the provisions. Senate majority leader Trent Lott threatened to shelve the bill and prevent a vote on it if the gun control measures were not removed. Senator Patrick J. Leahy, Democrat from Vermont stated: "The majority leader is paving the way to kill this bill and to shift the blame, mostly because of the gun related issues that have come up during this debate" (Bruni, May 18, 1999).

Surprisingly, the Senate eventually did pass some gun control measures. The main provision that was added was to make it mandatory that there be child safety locks on firearms. This moderate provision took significant compromise to be passed. However, on June 18, a similar bill was defeated in the Republican-controlled House. President Clinton stated: "The House leadership has gutted this bill in the dark of night. Our nation is waiting for Washington to pass a real law that keeps guns away from children and out of the hands of children. I call on Congress to stop playing politics and start living up to the responsibility to save lives." Some Republicans who were in favor of the bill's passage were upset by the NRA's influence on the party. Representative Christopher Shays, Republican from Connecticut, stated: "I hope in my lifetime the marriage between the NRA and my party ends in divorce. It's a bad marriage" (Bruni, June 19, 1999).

The battle for gun control legislation after the Columbine slaying demonstrates how contentious gun control legislation can be. The first thing of note is how fearful legislators were of confronting gun control legislation after the two major gun control bills that were passed in 1993 and 1994 led to the removal of many legislators in the following election. Gun control became taboo. The reason for the removal of legislators was because of the powerful lobbying effort by the NRA to remove anti-firearm Congressional members from office. The second thing to note is how closely the Republican Party and the NRA work together in proposing lenient gun control legislation and how effective they are in defeating restrictive gun control measures.

We now turn to a brief discussion of the two lenient pieces of gun control legislation that were created in the 109th Congress. The two pieces of legislation that were passed drew very little fanfare, but both were important. In fact, the gun control legislation that prevented firearms from being seized during period of crises was not even mentioned in the *New York Times*, and the gun control legislation that prevented firearms manufacturers from being held liable for their weapons being used in the commission of a crime only received one article of coverage. This just goes to demonstrate that lenient gun control legislation can be placed on the agenda and then formulated with very little interest from many people outside of Washington.

The last major focusing event to be discussed in the United States is the Virginia Tech Massacre. The Virginia Tech Massacre was the worst mass murder in the United States since the Killeen Texas slayings. Immediately following the shooting there was an outcry by gun control advocates for more gun control. However, there was not a significant desire by Congressional members to attempt to create new legislation. Senate Majority Leader Harry Reid, Democrat of Nevada, stated: "I hope there's not a rush to do anything. We need to take a deep breath." Even Senator Charles Schumer, an outspoken voice for more gun controls, stated that it was too early to discuss additional gun control measures (Eaton and Luo, April 18, 2007).

Even though Virginia Tech was a major focusing event, there was almost zero response from policy makers on the issue. Once again the fear of reprisal for voting for stricter gun control laws prevented gun control advocates from reacting. Even hardline gun control supporters stayed mute on the subject. Thus, after the 1994 election, restrictive gun control legislation has become taboo to most Democrats.

Conclusion: Important Factors in Determining Gun Control Policy in the United States

This chapter went into great detail about the public's attitudes toward firearms, it then switched to Congressional attention based on focusing events, and it finally concluded with a discussion of the reaction of politicians and interest group leaders to focusing events. I believe that the data discussed in this chapter lends credibility and support to some of the major themes of the book.

First, when we look at the public opinion in the United States, we find that over time the public has widely supported more gun controls. The data suggests that the majority public opinion has very little impact on the creation of new restrictive gun control legislation. The likely reason for this stems from Dahl's argument about apathetic majorities and intense minorities. The general public may support more restrictive gun control laws, but this has not been translated into increased support for the Brady Campaign and its goals to create these laws. Thus, public opinion in the United States is an insufficient explanatory variable in determining gun control policy outcomes.

The second major point comes from the examination of gun control agenda attention in Congress after a focusing event. The evidence suggests that focusing events do drive agenda attention; however, agenda attention very rarely results in gun control policy. The reason that agenda attention rarely leads to new gun control policy in the United States stems from three primary factors. The first of these factors is government structure. As mentioned earlier, government structure in the United States is designed to be inefficient. For this reason, only bills that are strongly supported by a single unified party or widely agreed upon as being necessary by both parties will ever become law. And when we consider the creation of new gun control laws, it rarely falls in to either of these categories.

The second major factor deals with political parties and their policy goals. When Republicans are in control, restrictive gun control legislation has never been created. The only time restrictive gun control legislation has been created was when the Democrats controlled both chambers of Congress and the Presidency. I would argue that the gun control legislation was only a modest or incremental change to gun control laws because of their limited goals.

The third and potentially most important factor in determining gun policy outcomes in the United States pertains to interest group power. Earlier when I discussed Congressional agenda attention to gun control policy, it was assumed that the NRA was influencing the outcome; however, it was hard to provide evidence of a direct linkage. Thus, it was important to obtain statements from politicians and interest groups discussing the primary movers and shakers in the gun control policy realm. Overwhelmingly, politicians from both parties stated that the NRA was the primary reason that gun control legislation was thwarted. When gun control legislation was created, in the Brady Bill and the Assault Weapons Ban, the politicians that brought the bill into being were punished severely in the 1994 election, which led to a Republican takeover of the House. And due to the 1994 election, Democrats tend to be, pardon the pun, very gun shy when dealing with gun control policy.

The data in Chapter 3 suggests that the primary reason that gun control legislation is not created after focusing events in the United States is because of NRA and its ability to target members of Congress. The multiple access points that allow the NRA to influence decision makers in Congress are due to the form of the presidential system in the United States. The data demonstrates that the primary factors that impact the creation or, more often, the defeat of legislation is the powerful status quo interest group, the NRA, and the institutional design of the American government which allows many points of access to attack and defeat legislation. Thus, the NRA and its influence are paramount in determining the outcome of gun control legislation at the national level in the United States.

Chapter 4

Canada: Violent Events Drive Change

Public Attitudes on Firearms in Canada

The public opinion data on gun control opinion in Canada was not as comprehensive as in the United States. The one polling service that I was able to use that had conducted multiple polls on the public's opinion on gun control was Ipsos-Reid, and their affiliate Angus-Reid. Unfortunately, Ipsos-Reid did not poll on gun control attitudes until the mid-1990s, when gun control became a salient issue in Canada, and they have not used any multi-year polls. However, the polls that they used provided us with a glimpse of the public's opinion during some of the most turbulent periods of gun policy debate in Canadian history.

The first poll that Ipsos-Reid conducted was between October 25 and November 1, 1995. A total of 1,503 adults were polled, with representative portions being polled from all provinces. The poll asked many broad political questions, but the question that was of importance to the gun control issue was: What were the biggest disappointments with the Liberal governments' accomplishments? Gun control was listed as the 8th biggest disappointment by Canadians; however, only 4% of the people who were polled found gun control to be the biggest failure, and the poll did not take into consideration if gun control was a disappointment because laws had been created or because laws had not been created.

In November of 1996, the polling question was revisited. A total of 1,506 adults were polled with representative portions being polled from all provinces. Gun control was once again considered to be a disappointment. This time it was considered to be the 10th largest disappointment of the Liberal-controlled Parliament; however, once again, only a small percentage of the population, 3% considered it to be the top problem.

Between the 9th and 15th of December 1996, Ipsos-Reid conducted its first poll that directly addressed attitudes on gun control policy. The national sample size was 1,504, with the sample size from each province being as follows: Ontario-526; Quebec-401; British Columbia 201; Alberta-135; Manitoba/Saskatchewan-121, and Atlantic Provinces-120. The poll sought to determine whether there was nationwide support for the new federal gun control legislation that was proposed in 1996, Bill C-68.

The poll found that 65% of Canadians surveyed expressed support for the federal government's new gun control legislation. Of the people polled, 44% were strongly in favor of the new legislation, and 21% were moderately in favor of the legislation. Of those that opposed the gun control legislation, 19% stated that they strongly opposed it, and 10% stated they were moderately opposed.

When the polling numbers are broken down by province, the location of the populations that support gun control and the populations that disfavor gun control are unsurprising. The eastern and more urban provinces were far more supportive of the federal government's gun control legislation, Ontario had 67% of its population in favor of the federal legislation, and 79% of Quebec's population were in favor of it, and 62% of Atlantic Provinces favored the legislation. The more rural western provinces were not as favorable toward the legislation; however, the public opinion of western provinces was not overwhelmingly opposed to gun control legislation. In Alberta 48% of the population favored the bill, with 46% opposing it. In Manitoba/Saskatchewan 51% of the population opposed the legislation. In British Columbia, 58% of the population actually favored the gun control legislation.

When the poll was studied based on gender, Ipsos-Reid found that the overwhelming support for the federal legislation was from women, with 73% of those polled being in favor of gun control; whereas, only 58% of males polled favored the legislation. Those who favored the gun control legislation were mostly from non-gun households, 73% of those polled who did not own a firearm strongly supported the gun control legislation. In contrast, 73% of those polled who owned firearms stated that they were against the federal legislation, with 56% of those stating that they were strongly against it.

This Ipsos-Reid poll provided a glimpse of Canadian attitudes toward gun control during the mid-1990s. Non-gun owners and people living in the eastern provinces, especially women, were strongly in favor of more restrictive gun control that was found in Bill C-68. However, western provinces were not as opposed to the legislation as often perceived by popular culture. Most western provinces were split almost 50/50 on supporting the Bill C-68. The polling data may demonstrate to us that Canadians from both eastern and western provinces may be more inclined to support federal gun control legislation than their counterparts in the United States.

In 1996, Bill C-68 was passed by Parliament and it led to the formulation and implementation of the Gun Registry. The previous poll demonstrates that the Gun Registry was widely supported at the time of its creation. However, six years later, in 2002, Ipsos-Reid once again sought Canadians' attitudes on the Gun Registry.

When the poll was taken in 2002, we find that the support for the Gun Registry had dwindled significantly. The primary question the poll asked the public was whether the Gun Registry in Canada should be scrapped, or completely eliminated. Fifty-three percent of Canadians believed that the Gun Registry should be scrapped; western provinces in particular were in favor of doing away with the entire program, with 67% of British Columbians, 67% of Albertans, 62% of residents of Manitoba and Saskatchewan. The desire to scrap the Gun Registry wasn't as high in eastern provinces with 48% of Ontarians, 45% of Quebecers, and 54% of residents of the Atlantic provinces favoring elimination of the bill.

When the polling numbers are examined further, we find that the greatest support for eliminating the Gun Registry was found in rural areas, with 62% of respondents favoring scrapping the Gun Registry, in contrast to the 51% of respondents living in urban areas who favored scrapping it. Also, men were far more likely to favor the elimination of the Gun Registry, with 60% of men and only 47% of women desiring that it should be eliminated.

Canadians fervently supported the Gun Registry when it was first proposed and implemented after a series of major focusing events. However, after six years of no major focusing events, and the Gun Registry costing Canadian tax payers a huge sums of money, support for it had declined.

In 2004, Ipsos-Reid once again polled Canadians on the Gun Registry. Fifty-two percent of Canadians believed that the Gun Registry should be scrapped, with the largest number of those favoring the elimination of the bill coming from the Western provinces, with 64% of British Columbians, 64% of residents from Saskatchewan/Manitoba, 57% of residents from Alberta. Eastern provinces for the most part still held a slim advantage in those desiring to keep the Gun Registry in place, with 48% of residents of Quebec, and 45% of the residents of Ontario favoring the elimination of the Gun Registry. However, 61% of residents from Atlantic Canadian provinces favored elimination of the Gun Registry. Demographically, those living in rural areas were more likely to favor the elimination of the Gun Registry, 64%, to only 49% of urban Canadians. Men were also still more likely to favor the dissolution of the Gun Registry with 58% favoring its elimination to only 46% of women.

In 2006, Ipsos-Reid again polled Canadians on their opinions of the Gun Registry. On May 15, 2006, 54% of Canadians believed the Gun Registry was badly organized, was not working properly, and should be scrapped. However, 67% of Canadians believed that some sort of gun registration should be maintained, but not the current system of 2006. Western provinces still maintained the largest percentages of Canadians who believed that the Gun Registry should be scrapped, with 72% of residents of Alberta, 71% of residents of Saskatchewan/Manitoba, and 62% of residents from British Columbia sharing this opinion. In the eastern provinces, 60% of residents of Ontario, 55% of residents of the Atlantic Provinces and 44% of residents of Quebec were unhappy with the Gun Registry in its 2006 form. Demographically, 62% of men believed that the Gun Registry should be scrapped, to only 48% of women thinking that way.

When the new Conservative government took control of Parliament in 2006, Ipsos-Reid asked Canadians: "Should the Conservative keep in place some sort of system that makes gun owners across the country register their firearms." Sixty-seven percent of Canadians believed that the Conservatives should keep in place some sort of system to register firearms, whereas 31% felt that all gun registration should be eliminated. The largest supporters for maintaining some form of Gun Registry were found in Ontario, 71% of those polled, and Quebec, 76% of those polled. The residents of Saskatchewan/Manitoba and Alberta were the most against maintaining a Gun Registry, with 47% of residents of Saskatchewan/Manitoba and 41% of residents from Alberta strongly opposing it.

The 2007 Virginia Tech massacre led the Ipsos-Reid poll to conduct a poll asking Canadians if they thought an event like that could take place in Canada. The poll revealed that 64% of Canadians believed that the same kind of campus shooting could take place in Canada. Seventy-four percent of women polled believed an event like the one seen at Virginia Tech could happen in Canada, as opposed to 55% of men believing a similar event could take place.

Ipsos-Reid took the question a step further and asked: Is there any way to prevent an event like this from occurring. Sixty-three percent of Canadians did not believe any action can be taken to prevent this sort of tragedy. Ipsos-Reid also asked if Canadians thought that the Gun Registry would help prevent this type of incident. Sixty-five percent of Canadians polled believed that the Gun Registry would have no impact in stopping such an event. Men are also more likely than women to believe that the Gun Registry would have little to no impact, with 69% of men feeling that way compared, to 60% of women.

The last two public opinion polls come from Ipsos-Reid affiliate Angus-Reid. The January 2008 poll investigated whether a countrywide ban on handguns would be effective in lowering crime. The poll found that 78% of Canadians believe that there is a serious gun violence problem in Canada. However, when asked if there should be a total ban on handguns, 45% of the population thought there should be a ban while 46% disagreed with a handgun ban. The poll also asked if Canadians thought a handgun ban would be effective in deterring crime. Forty-nine percent of Canadians thought that the ban would be effective in deterring crime; however, 49% also thought that the ban would be ineffective in deterring crime.

Although the public opinion data on gun control in Canada was hard to find and the data doesn't cover my entire period of study; it does give us some useful insights on how Canadians view the gun control issue. In the mid-1990s after there were a multitude of major focusing events in Canada, the majority of Canadians favored stricter gun control. However, as time went by and there were no more major focusing events in Canada and the Gun Registry became cumbersome, wasteful, and widely viewed as ineffective, public opinion on the Gun Registry and gun control as a whole changed.

The polling data demonstrates that Canadians do not favor restrictive gun control legislation as often as perceived in popular culture. Canadians from the more populous portions of Canada, tend to favor more restrictive gun control. Women and those people who were from non-gun owning households also tended to be more supportive of these gun laws. Men and individuals from rural areas and from the more conservative western provinces were more inclined to support less government involvement. Thus, there does appear to be a cultural divide in Canada on gun control, and that restrictive gun control is not as unanimously supported as may be perceived by common knowledge.

The next portion of this section goes into a discussion of the study of public opinion on gun control that was conducted by Mauser and Margolis (1992). Their findings are similar to mine in that they do not believe that public opinion on gun control in the United States and Canada are radically different.

Mauser and Margolis: Their Study of Canadian and American Public Opinion on Guns

Mauser and Margolis (1992) argued that the public opinion on gun control in both the United States and Canada was similar. They found that large majorities of the publics from both countries support moderate gun control laws. Mauser and Margolis suggest that the differences in attitudes on gun control in Canada are often attributed to what scholars assume as common knowledge rather than cold hard facts.

Some of the interesting statistics that Mauser and Margolis mention in the body of their work is that in Canada, over 50% of the population believes that Canadians have a right to bear arms. They also found that 79% of Canadians and 86% of Americans agreed that only law-abiding citizens would be impacted by stricter gun control legislation and that the laws would have little impact on crime. However, on the issue of handguns, Canadians as a whole are more willing to support far more stringent controls than their American counterparts.

The following figures and tables were taken from Mauser's and Margolis's (1992) work. They allow us to see some comparison between the two countries (Table 4.1). Table 4.1 asks: "Do you favor or oppose a law which would require a person to obtain a police permit before he or she could buy a firearm?"

Table 4.1 demonstrates that in 1977 large majorities of both Canadians and Americans favored obtaining a license from the police to be able to acquire a firearm. However, by 1990, the number of Canadians who favored this had increased by 7%; whereas, their American counterparts had decreased by 14%. Nonetheless, the data demonstrates that

Table 4.1 Do you favor or oppose a law which would require a person to obtain a police permit before he or she could buy a firearm?

	Canada		United States	
	Gallup (1977)	**ICCS (1990)**	**Caddell (1978)**	**ICCS (1990)**
Favor (%)	85	92	82	68
Oppose (%)	12	7	14	29
No opinion (%)	3	1	5	3
N	*1,500*	*387*	*1500*	*334*

Source: Mauser and Margolis 1992.

large percentages of Canadians and Americans favor requiring a license before an individual can legally obtain a handgun.

Table 4.2 asked the question: "Do you believe that you, as a citizen, have a right to own a gun?"

Table 4.2 demonstrates that a majority of both Canadians and American believe that there is a right granted to them to own a firearm. The percentage is far higher in the United States than in Canada, with the biggest discrepancy being when non-firearms owners in Canada are compared with non-firearms owners in the United States. Non-firearms owners in Canada were far less likely to support the opinion that there was a right to own them.

Tables 4.3 and 4.4 investigate firearms laws and their impact on criminal activity.

Table 4.2 Do you believe that you, as a citizen, have a right to own a gun?

	Canada (1990)			USA (1990)		
	Total	**Firearms**	**Non-firearms**	**Total**	**Firearms**	**Non-firearms**
	Sample	*Owners*	*Owners*	*Sample*	*Owners*	*Owners*
Yes (%)	56	80	45	86	96	75
No (%)	44	20	55	14	4	25
N	*386*	*121*	*260*	*339*	*160*	*170*

Source: Mauser and Margolis 1992.

Table 4.3 Would you say there are already too many laws governing the possession of firearms, the present laws are about right, or that we need more laws?

	Mauser	**ICCS**	**DMI**	**ICCS**
	BC **(1988)**	**Canada** **(1990)**	**USA** **(1978)**	**USA** **(1990)**
Too many laws (%)	6	3	13	12
About right (%)	37	34	41	38
Need more laws (%)	45	60	44	45
NA/DK (%)	12	3	2	5
N	*405*	*393*	*1500*	*344*

Source: Mauser and Margolis 1992.

Table 4.4   If there were more firearms
laws, do you think the crime rate would
decrease, increase, or stay the same as
it is now?

	Canada	USA
Decrease (%)	42	30
Stay the same (%)	52	55
Increase (%)	8	15
N	380	323

Source: Mauser and Margolis (1992).

When we look at Table 4.3 we find that small percentages of both
countries think that there were too many gun control laws in place.
The percentages of both countries who found that the amount of gun
control laws were about right were nearly identical, with only slightly
more Americans saying that gun control laws were about right than
Canadians. The one figure that is the most interesting to me is the number of Canadians who thought that there should be more gun control
laws. In 1988, the number of Canadian who thought there should be
more laws were nearly identical to their counterparts in the United
States from 1978 and 1990. However, in 1990 the number of Canadians
who favor more gun control laws increased by 15%; whereas, the number of Americans who favored more gun control laws stayed static at
45%. I would argue that the primary reason there was this huge jump
was because of the Montreal Massacre and the push by many to create
new gun control laws. If there were no major focusing event present, I
would suggest that the number of Canadians who favored stricter gun
control laws would probably look more like the 1988 numbers than the
1990 numbers.

Table 4.4 demonstrates that Canadians and Americans for the most
part share similar views on whether new gun control would have much
impact on crime rates. More Canadians than Americans thought that
crime would decrease; whereas, more Americans than Canadians
thought that crime would increase. However, the large majority of both
populations thought that more firearms laws would have no impact on
gun control.

The information discussed above is useful in that it provides us with an
understanding of gun policy attitudes in Canada in the late 1970s, and
in the 1980s. This information demonstrates that American attitudes on

gun control policy and Canadian attitudes on gun control policy vary very little. However, the biggest detriment to the Mauser and Margolis study is that it takes place before the true birth of the gun control movement in Canada. The Coalition for Gun Control was still in its infancy, and the majority of the significant gun control laws that would eventually be proposed were not in the consciousness of Canadians. But even with this drawback to their study, they make some conclusions that I find to be applicable to my study.

Like Mauser and Margolis, I find that public opinions on gun control in the United States and Canada are both similar to one another. Thus, it makes it difficult to use public opinion as an explanatory variable for the differences between gun control policy in the United States and Canada.

Section Two: Bill Proposals and Bill Formulation in Canada

This section is divided into three. The first discusses government gun bill proposals when there was a right-of-center party in control of Parliament. The two right-of-center parties that held power were the Conservatives and the Progressive Conservatives. The second discusses government gun bill proposals when there was a left-of-center government in power, the primary party being the Liberals. The third discusses the government gun bills that were proposed and whether the bill became law or failed.

Right-of-Center Parties

One thing that must be noted in discussion of government gun bill proposals in Canada, not just for right-of-center parties, but for all parties, is that the number of gun bills proposed is drastically fewer than in the United States. This has to do with the difference between an efficient parliamentary system and an inefficient presidential democracy.

Like the United States, I broke government gun bill proposals down into four different categories: overall number of government gun bills proposed, number of government gun bills proposed when there is a major focusing event, number of government gun bills proposed in Parliaments that follow Parliaments that contained a major focusing

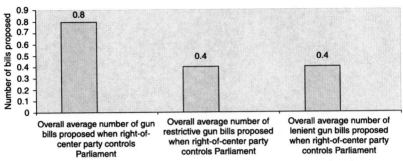

FIGURE 4.1 Average number of gun bill proposed when right-of-center party controls Parliament 1963–2008

event, and the number of government gun bills proposed when there are no major focusing events. Also like the United States, bills that were proposed that related to gun crimes and sentencing were not included. These government bills are not targeting guns specifically; rather they focus on punishments for crimes, and are generally proposed by right-of-center parties.

Figure 4.1 examines the overall number of government gun bills proposed when right-of-center parties are in power.

Figure 4.1 demonstrates that when Conservatives are in control of Parliament very few gun bills were proposed. There is an average of only 0.8 gun bills proposed, with 0.4 of those being lenient in nature, and 0.4 being restrictive in nature. This very low number is not completely surprising considering that the total number of government bills proposed in Parliament is far lower than proposed in the US Congress; however, less than one bill being proposed a Parliament still seems quite low.

Figure 4.2 examines the number of gun bills proposed when there is a major focusing event and right-of-center parties control Parliament.

Figure 4.2 demonstrates that when there is a major focusing event, the number of government gun bills proposed more than doubles, and that no lenient gun bills are proposed. However, the data in Figure 4.2 is hard to generalize since the only time that the Conservatives controlled Parliament and there were major focusing events was in the late 1980s and early 1990s during such major focusing events as the Montreal Massacre. It is still interesting to note that right-of-center parties in Canada actively pursued creating new restrictive gun control legislation and no lenient gun control legislation was proposed at all to counter the restrictive measures. This still suggests that major focusing events do impact gun bill agenda setting.

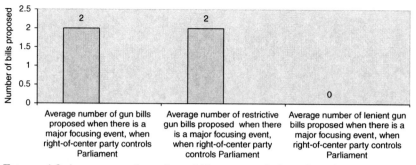

FIGURE 4.2 Average number of gun bills proposed when there is a major focusing event, and right-of-center party controls Parliament 1963–2008

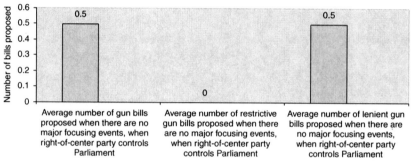

FIGURE 4.3 Average number of gun bills proposed when there are no major focusing events and right-of-center party controls Parliament 1963–2008

Since there has not been a time when a right-of-center party controlled Parliament that followed a Parliament that contained a major focusing event, Figure 4.3 examines gun bill proposals when there are no major focusing events and a right-of-center party controls Parliament.

In Figure 4.3, we find that when there are no major focusing events, there are no restrictive gun bills proposed by right-of center parties. However, there are lenient gun bills being proposed, albeit rarely. The data suggests that when there are no major focusing events to sway public opinion, right-of-center parties do not seek to create new gun control measures in Canada.

When comparing the data in Figure 4.2 with the data in Figure 4.3 it is clear that major focusing events greatly influence the nature of gun bill proposals by right-of-center parties. We find that the only time restrictive gun control bills are proposed in Canada are when there are major focusing events. On the other side, when there are no major focusing events, no restrictive government gun bills are proposed. The number of lenient government gun bills proposed when right-of-center parties govern is extremely low. During times of major focusing events, there are no lenient government gun control bills being proposed, and when there are no major focusing events there is on average only one lenient government gun control bill being proposed every other Parliament. This suggests that pro-gun groups have a difficult time in getting their lenient bill proposals on the agenda.

Left-of-Center Parties

Like right-of-center parties in Canada, left-of-center parties do not propose great amounts of restrictive gun control legislation. Figure 4.4 examines the average number of bill proposals when left-of-center parties control Parliament.

The data demonstrates that gun control legislation is not introduced at high levels when left-of-center parties are in control. There is only an average of one gun bill proposed every other Parliament. What is also interesting to note is that from 1963 to 2008 there were zero lenient gun bill proposed when left-of-center parties were in control. The data suggests gun control legislation is not necessarily a hot topic on the agenda in Canadian Parliament. Is there a time when more gun control bills are proposed? Figures 4.5–4.7 break down the numbers.

Figure 4.5 looks at gun bill introductions when there are major focusing events and Parliament is controlled by left-of-center parties.

The data in Figure 4.5 demonstrates that when there is a major focusing event the number of gun bills proposed increase by 100%, and the

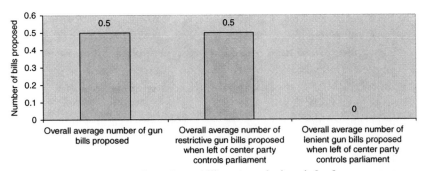

FIGURE 4.4 Average number of gun bill proposed when left-of-center party controls Parliament 1963–2008

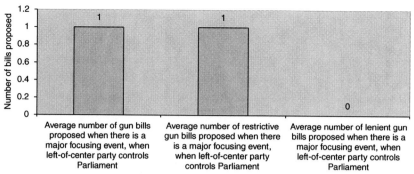

FIGURE 4.5 Average number of gun bills proposed when there is a major focusing event, and left-of-center party controls Parliament 1963–2008

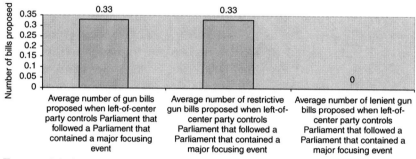

FIGURE 4.6 Average number of gun bills proposed in Parliaments that follow Parliaments that contained a major focusing event, left-of-center party control of Parliament 1963–2008

number of restrictive bills proposed increase by 100%. The total number of bills introduced is not a very large number, only one bill, but considering that Parliaments tend to be much more efficient than presidential systems it is not surprising that only one large and expansive bill would be proposed as opposed to many smaller bills like we see in the United States. The data in this figure demonstrates that there is definitely an increase in bill introductions when there is a major focusing event and left-of-center parties control Parliament.

In order to understand if there is a lagged effect in agenda attention to focusing events, Figure 4.6 examines gun bill introductions in Parliaments that follow those that had a major focusing event, and a left-of-center party controls Parliament.

The data in Figure 4.6 shows that the number of gun bills introduced in Parliaments that follow those that had a major focusing event

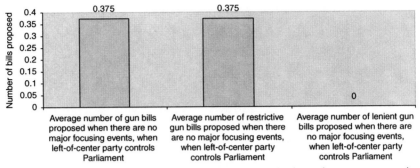

FIGURE 4.7 Average number of gun bills proposed when there are no major focusing events, left-of-center party control of Parliament 1963–2008

is quite low. The data demonstrates that only about one in every three Parliaments proposes new gun control legislation. This is not terribly surprising however. In the United States, a Congressional term is only two years and is a relatively short period of time for new gun control legislation to be created. Parliamentary terms, on the other hand, may last for years. This means that the data in Figure 4.6 is probably not as useful as the American counterpart figures in Chapter 3.

Figure 4.7 focuses on when there are no major focusing events and left-of-center parties control Parliament.

The data demonstrates that when there are no major focusing events and left-of-center parties control Parliament, there are still very few gun control bills proposed. Only about one bill proposed every three Parliaments. This suggests that when there is no major focusing event, gun control legislation does not often get on the agenda.

The data in this section demonstrates that gun control agenda attention is at its highest when there are major focusing events. The number of bills proposed when left-of-center parties control Parliament is still very low, but I believe this is due to the fact that the Canadian Parliament proposes less legislation of all types than the United States. However, even with that, gun control legislation seems to be fairly low on the agenda in Canada.

Canadian Bills Proposed and/or Formulated

This section analyzes the government gun bills that were proposed in Canada between 1963 and 2008. Table 4.5 splits the government gun bills that have been introduced in Canada for the time period 1963–2008.

Table 4.5 Government gun bills: 1963–2008

Parliament	Bill	Type	Party in control of Parliament	Was there a focusing event	Did it become law?
28th	C-150	Restrictive	Liberal	Yes	Yes
30th	C-83	Restrictive	Liberal	No	No
30th	C-51	Restrictive	Liberal	No	Yes
34th	C-80	Restrictive	Progressive Conservative	Yes	No
34th	C-17	Restrictive	Progressive Conservative	Yes	Yes
35th	C-68	Restrictive	Liberal	Yes	Yes
37th	C-15	Restrictive	Liberal	No	Yes
39th	C-21	Lenient	Conservative	No	No
39th	C-24	Lenient	Conservative	No	No

Of the nine government bills that were proposed between 1963 and 2008, four of them were created in response to major focusing events. Of the nine bills that were proposed, two were lenient in nature and it is unsurprising that they were not proposed during Parliaments that contained a major focusing event. This means that four, and arguably five (Bill C-17 was created in an attempt to tweak the legislation created by Bill C-68), of seven restrictive government gun bills were proposed in response to a major focusing event. If we include Bill C-17, this means that four of five restrictive government bills were proposed in response to major focusing events became law, an 80% success rate. Of the restrictive gun bills proposed when there were no major focusing events, there was only a 50% success rate.

Five of the seven restrictive gun bills were proposed by the Liberal Party. Two of these restrictive gun bills were in direct response to major focusing events, Bill C-150 and Bill C-68. Both of these bills became law. Bill C-17, as mentioned above, was created to improve upon Bill C-68, thus it was created indirectly by a focusing event. This leads to two restrictive gun bills being proposed when there were no major focusing events and a left-of-center party was in power, Bills C-83, and C-51. Bill C-83 failed to become law, and C-51 a restrictive bill, but less restrictive than C-83, was then created. Thus, three of four restrictive government gun bills that became law in Canada were in response to major focusing events in Canada.

Only two of the seven restrictive government gun bills were proposed by right-of-center parties. Bill C-80 was the first response by the Progressive Conservative government of Prime Minister Mulroney, but after it was defeated, government Bill C-17 was created, and it eventually became law. Thus, the only piece of restrictive gun control legislation that was created by right-of-center parties was in direct response to arguably the worst focusing event in Canada, the Montreal Massacre.

Section Three: The Montreal Massacre and Conservative Control of Parliament in the Early 1990s

The Montreal Massacre was perpetrated by Marc Lepine on December 6, 1989. Lepine specifically targeted women in his attack. This event triggered the birth of the Coalition for Gun Control, a feminist group and arguably the most influential gun control interest group in Canada, and its influence has led to the creation of significant restrictive gun control legislation in Canada since 1989.

Two days after the shooting, December 8, 1989, members of the opposition parties, the New Democrats and the Liberals, began immediately calling for new gun control legislation. The Conservative government in power at the time was hesitant to react. Justice Minister Douglas Lewis stated: "They (semi-automatics) are used for peaceful purposes, they are used by hunters, they are used to shoot at targets, but what we've been after are automatic weapons, the weapon that is originally designed, manufactured, assembled to fire in an automatic mode, which they convert to semis to get them into the country and can be converted back. There is absolutely no peaceful use for an automatic Uzi . . . You don't shoot targets with them because there is nothing left of the target." Lewis went on to state that legislation would not protect Canadians from insanity (Cleroux and McInnes, December 8, 1989).

On December 9, 1989 other members of Parliament including some Progressive Conservative backbenchers called for the outright banning of all semiautomatic weapons. Justice Minister Douglas stated that he had been dealing with interest groups on both sides of the issue in order to bring forth an amendment to the gun control laws that would eliminate the importation of automatic weapons to Canada. Firearms advocates were concerned that a knee jerk reaction to the Montreal rampage would result in the banning of automatic and semiautomatic weapons (Fraser, December 9, 1989).

The Montreal Massacre induced a nearly instant reaction by members of Parliament and interest groups. In three-day time period, members of both parties were calling for new and restrictive gun control legislation.

On December 11, 1989, Prime Minister Brian Mulroney stated: "I think that it's a very serious and unacceptable matter. The manner in which society, almost in a cavalier manner, tolerates the concept of violence, and violence against women, is profoundly unacceptable." Mulroney also expressed displeasure for provinces not accepting gun control measures that had been proposed in the past (*Globe and Mail,* December 11, 1989).

The role of the western provinces in retarding gun control legislation is a recurring theme. Brown-John in a study on the Gun Registry discusses the political leanings of provinces. The western provinces are more right leaning and generally favor less restrictive gun control legislation. The western provinces that are typically very anti-gun control legislation are: Alberta, Manitoba, Saskatchewan, British Columbia, and rural portions of Ontario. However, the majority of Ontario and Quebec, which contains a majority of Canada's population, are generally more liberal and favor more restrictive gun control legislation (Brown-John 2003). The battle against restrictive gun control legislation by western provinces is more pronounced later in the chapter.

On March 17, 1990 new justice minister Kim Campbell stated that new gun control legislation would soon be proposed. On June 26, 1990, new gun control legislation was in fact proposed; Bill C-80 was a direct response to the Montreal Massacre that had happened a few months prior. The new gun bill took a tougher stance on military assault weapons, and tightened rules for the ownership of firearms. However, a ban that would affect hunting rifles and semiautomatic weapons was avoided (*Globe and Mail,* June 26, 1990).

A year after the Montreal Massacre, the debate over new gun control legislation intensified. Many opposition party MPs and even some Conservative MPs, mainly women from Ontario and Quebec, became frustrated that new gun control legislation was not created. Bill C-80 had been delayed and nearly killed by some Conservative opposition, but with the anniversary of the Montreal Massacre, support for the bill once again grew (Fraser, December 7, 1990).

The NFA, Canada's most influential pro-gun group, was not mentioned at all publicly until early 1991, when opposition party members argued that the reason that the Conservatives and Justice Minister Kim Campbell had not already turned Bill C-80 in to law was due to the gun lobby. Wendy Cukier of Canadians for Gun Control, the precursor to the Coalition for Gun Control, stated: "The gun lobby often attempts to trivialize gun control lobbyists as a bunch of feminists." Due to the fact that Marc Lepine specifically targeted women in his attack, the gun control movement in Canada was not only about guns, but also about preventing violence against women. This is a stark contrast to the United States, where gun control has never taken on a feminist perspective. Many women legislators, including Conservatives, would not support the Conservative Party in allowing Bill C-80 to die. Progressive Conservative MP Pierette Venne stated: "If there had been more of us women on the committee, I'm convinced the report would have been different." This comment was her response to a report from a Conservative committee that had stated that there was not much need for more stringent gun control laws (Delacourt, February 8, 1991).

Justice Minister Campbell took offense to the accusations that she was planning on weakening the gun control legislation. She stated: "I just wanted to nip in the bud the suggestion that I have any intention of weakening my firearms legislation. I have not weakened my commitment, I have not buckled under to any lobby, I have not been intimidated by any soul, and I don't know how much more clearly I can say that." Her comments were in response to wide-ranging predictions that Bill C-80 would fail (Wilson, February 9, 1991).

After nearly a year of deliberation, Bill C-80 did in fact fail to become law. The fact that a government bill did not become law is somewhat surprising. As mentioned in Chapter 2, there is generally strict party discipline in Canada when it comes to voting. Joseph Wearing (1998), in a study of dissent within Parliament, found that on average less than 10% of the party will dissent with a government bill, and the percentage of those dissenting is often as low as to 2–3%. However, Wearing states that the two key issues where MPs are most likely to dissent with their party are bills that deal with gay rights and gun control (Wearing 1998). Wearing's discussion is interesting because it demonstrates that MPs are conscious of their ridings, and may vote against the party. Gun control and gay rights are both contentious issues and it is unsurprising that MPs might be more likely to vote their conscience than vote with their party on these issues, especially, if they represent a riding that has particularly strong leanings. Thus, the fact that a bill that impacted many Conservatives and their gun-owning constituency was defeated is not as surprising as it might have been to see some other government bill fail.

However, even with the death of Bill C-80, gun control was still a salient issue in the Conservative Parliament in early 1991. On March 17, 1991, after 500,000 signatures petitioning for new gun control legislation were presented to the House of Commons, Justice Minister Campbell stated that the recommendations of the petitioners were "sensible and helpful." Campbell stated that a new gun bill was being drafted that would be easier to push through the House of Commons and would also be stricter than the gun control legislation proposed in Bill C-80 (York, March 27, 1991).

On May 30, 1991, new gun control legislation was introduced. Bill C-17 was a response to the failure of Bill C-80 to make it out of committee. Bill C-17 was weaker in several areas than Bill C-80; however, to get the support of many western Conservative MPs, some compromises had to be made. Wendy Cukier, President of the Coalition for Gun Control, stated: "Most of what we've heard would be bad. The whole process has been oriented toward appeasing the gun lobby and the Alberta MPs. Everybody underestimated the power of the gun lobby." Even with the weakening of the proposed bill, many experts believed that the bill would still have difficult trouble going through the Conservative-controlled House of Commons and the continued presence of the gun lobby. David Tomlinson, president of the NFA stated that he expected the bill to make "some minor improvements" but he would continue to criticize the government for going ahead with the bill (York, May 30, 1991).

On June 1, 1991, lobbyists from both sides of the issue commented on the gun control legislation. Gun control advocates considered the bill to be far too weak; whereas, gun rights proponents stated that the bill was misguided. President of the NFA David Tomlinson stated that he was confident that the bill would be killed. He suggested that the previous gun control bill had been "left upside-down in a ditch because of strong opposition from thousands of gun owners." Tomlinson stated that Deputy Prime Minister Donald Mazankowski, who represented a rural portion of Alberta, was the gun lobby's biggest supporter and gun supporters were lobbying him extensively to get the new legislation killed (York, June 1, 1991).

On November 7, 1991, Bill C-17 was voted into law. After the bill was approved, Justice Minister Kim Campbell explained the uniqueness of the Canadian situation in regard to gun control: "Canada has its own firearms culture. We have many, many, many law abiding Canadians who own firearms, and that is a very important part of our cultural tradition. We also have a culture that is non-violent, concerned about public safety and has respect for public security." The comments appeared to be discussing the comparison between gun control legislation in Canada versus gun control legislation in the United States. It definitely was the case when Liberal MP Russell MacLellan stated: "Our culture here is not dependent on firearms as it is south of the border."

Not everyone voted for the legislation, Progressive Conservative John MacDougall was one of the dissenters. He stated: "We're against the fact that legislation is being put in against law-abiding citizens. There's an awfully large community out there that for years have handled guns. We seem to be the ones affected with this legislation, we're not dealing with the criminal aspect" (Fraser, November 7, 1991). The fact that there were several Progressive Conservatives that voted against the bill would be surprising in most instances. However, after considering the previous discussion by Wearing, it is less of a surprise to see several Conservatives, especially those representing rural ridings, voting against the legislation.

Coalition for Gun Control representative, Wendy Cukier, called the legislation modest, but a major victory for a loose coalition over special interest groups, such as gun owners, who had shown immense power in the United States. Cukier stated: "The gun lobby applied its back room political pressure and nearly convinced the Conservatives to stack the legislative process against us. But, because the issue was in the public eye, focused by the Montreal massacre, and attempts to weaken the legislation were publicized, all three party leaders pressed the majority of their MPs into supporting the bill" (Howard, November 8, 1991).

On December 6, 1991 the Senate signed the gun bill into law. Senator Joyce Fairbairn stated: "This is the strongest response we could give to all those who will remember the second anniversary of the Montreal tragedy and all the other lives which have been so cruelly ended by violence with guns." The bill was rushed through the Senate to ensure that it would gain royal assent before the second anniversary of the slayings. Fairbairn also went on to state: "This bill is not the end of the issue. It is a foundation upon which we must build steadily" (York, December 6, 1991).

The Montreal Massacre and the subsequent battle between western Conservatives and gun lobbyist with women, liberal parties, and eastern Conservatives eventually led to the creation of new gun control legislation. The Montreal Massacre was the event that triggered the creation of the Coalition for Gun Control and ultimately new restrictive legislation. The power of the gun lobby and its right-of-center allies in western Canada were able to initially prevent the creation of gun control legislation, Bill

C-80. However, the powerful movement by women, left-of-center parties that included the Liberals and Bloc Quebecois, and a defection by many Conservatives, in particular women, led to the gun lobby being trumped and the second piece of gun control legislation that was proposed, Bill C-17, to become law. The powerful women's movement that sought gun control became the Coalition for Gun Control, and its power to influence gun control legislation after focusing events continued to increase through the 1990s.

After the 1991 legislation was created, there was a continued drive by politicians and interest groups to create more gun control legislation. Many thought that the legislation created by the Conservatives had been too weak. On August 24, even more fuel was added to the fire when a disgruntled university professor at Concordia University in Montreal killed two faculty members and wounded three other university employees (two more of those wounded would eventually die after the event). The firearm that was used by the professor was a legally obtained and legally owned firearm.

The shooting brought an immediate response from gun control interest groups. Heidi Rathjen, executive director of the Coalition for Gun Control, stated that the shooting would renew the call for tougher gun control. She stated: "One thing is clear: Without a gun he couldn't have done what he did. Definitely, easy access to guns is a factor that has to be looked at in this case . . . Canadians should not tolerate that restricted, concealable weapons are easy to obtain" (Gibbon and Picard, August 25, 1992).

Professor Fabrikant was granted a handgun permit even after several members of the Concordia faculty had asked that he be denied a permit because of his erratic behavior. The permit that he requested was denied; however, two permits requested by his wife were granted and these were the firearms used in the slaying. Justice Minister Kim Campbell stated that new gun control legislation would look into the need for police to have medical and psychiatric files of applicants. And gun control advocates stated that loopholes such as the ones used for Professor Fabrikant to obtain the firearms demonstrated the immediate need for the creation of new gun control legislation in Canada (Picard, August 27, 1992).

On September 23, 1992, the rector of Concordia University Patrick Kenniff told the *Globe and Mail* that the university was going to be launching a campaign for an outright ban on handguns in Canada. Kenniff stated: "There is no redeeming feature to the possession of handguns in this country, no redeeming argument for their possession. Our goal is to secure the outright prohibition of handguns in Canada." The support for the campaign was backed by many gun control proponents in Canada (Picard, September 23, 1992).

The Montreal Massacre and the Concordia University slayings put significant pressure on the Conservatives to consider gun control legislation. On April 28, 1993, Patrick Kenniff, the rector of Concordia University, demanded to know the stance on gun control policy that the Conservatives who were running for the prime ministership held. Kenniff stated: "We think this is an issue of interest to all Canadians, one that should be debated not only in the party leadership campaign but during the next federal election campaign." Kenniff and his supporters were able to obtain over 120,000 signatures to the petition seeking the banning of handguns (Picard, April 28, 1993).

In late 1993, the Progressive Conservatives lost control of Parliament to the Liberals. The next section of the books examines bill proposals and focusing events during the Liberal control of Parliament in the mid-1990s.

The 1990s and Liberal Control of Parliament

Immediately after the Concordia shooting there had been a heavy push by gun control advocates to create new legislation; however, the Conservatives did not attempt to push the agenda for new gun controls. But, the Liberal Party promised during its campaign that one of the primary issues on what it would change policy was gun control (*Globe and Mail*, October 5, 1993).

On December 31, 1993 the provisions of Bill C-17 came into effect. Ernest Sopsich, executive director of the Canadian Shooting Federation commented on the phasing in of Bill C-17: "The only people who will be affected, the people who will lose out, are the law-abiding, legitimate shooters, collectors, and hunters. The people who do not have the legal right to own a firearm because their intent is owning one for criminal acts, those people don't give a sweet damn about firearm laws" (*Globe and Mail*, December 31, 1993).

On April 5, 1994, another major focusing event occurred. Georgina Leimonis was killed with a sawed off shotgun during a robbery at a Just Desserts restaurant in Toronto. Though the event involved just a single individual, it sparked a hailstorm of intense media coverage which sparked an outcry for more gun control legislation. By April 12, 1994, the

Metro Toronto Police Services Board had urged Ottawa to tighten provisions of the Criminal Code on the use of firearms during the commission of offenses. Gun control groups also began demanding for tougher gun control laws (Moon, April 12, 1994).

On April 12, 1994 Justice Minister Allan Rock stated that a total ban on gun ownership was being considered except by the police and soldiers. Justice Minister Rock stated: "I came to Ottawa in November of last year with the firm belief that the only people in this country who should have guns are police officers and soldiers. That is my personal belief, very strongly held . . . Above all, I do not want to find Canada falling into a cycle where people believe that they have to acquire a weapon for the protection of themselves." Minister Rock stated he wasn't sure when new gun control measures would be introduced, but he planned to introduce them soon and one of the major provisions would be the complete banning of firearms in cities (Delacourt, April 12, 1994).

On May 16, 1994, Prime Minister Jean Chretien promised that tough new gun control laws would be created. He stated that the laws would be "as strong as possible." Chretien went on to state: "Tough talk is easy. What Canadians want and we have to provide is tough action. I hope we have the support of all parties for this tough gun control" (Howard, May 16, 1994).

On August 26, 1994, Justice Minister Allan Rock first mentioned that the universal registration of 7 million firearms in the country would make Canada a safer place. Registration of all handguns and restricted weapons was already a law in Canada; however, the legislation that Minister Rock suggested would require the registration of all rifles and shotguns as well. One of the biggest arguments against the registration of all weapons was the cost. However, Minister Rock believed that the cost would be countered by the larger savings to society due to the increased safety and lower criminality. Rock stated: "Imagine a system that can be operated at minimal cost with minimal imposition . . ." (Picard, August 26, 1994).

On October 22, 1994, Prime Minister Chretien reinforced the opinion of Justice Minister Rock when he stated that a federal Firearms Registry needed to be put into place. He stated: "I believe we have to force everybody to register their guns. We register all cars. What's wrong with registering all guns?" (Winsor and Tu, October 22, 1994).

On November 26, 1994, the *Globe and Mail*, discussed the inability of the Canadian gun lobby to prevent legislation, unlike its counterpart in the United States. The article stated that the gun lobby in Canada used its most vigorous opposition ever in 1994 in an attempt to prevent the Gun Registry proposal from being placed on the agenda. However, the gun lobby in Canada has continually been thwarted by the Coalition for Gun Control. Reasons for the failure of the gun lobby in Canada were due to the lack of the NRA's unity, network of contacts, and single-minded resolve. Jules Sobrian, founder of the Responsible Firearms Coalition of Ontario stated: "The gun lobby right now is an unarmed Goliath. There might be seven million of us, but we cannot do anything." Sobrian added: "You might say it's a movement waiting for a leader. The leaders are fellows who have a lot of personality, but for some reason their tactics don't work. They are mostly pacifists and don't want to be identified as rednecks with guns" (Makin, November 26, 1994).

On December 1, 1994, the Liberals and Justice Minister Allan Rock finally proposed the gun control bill that advocates had been awaiting. Rock proposed to introduce mandatory prison sentences of at least four years for serious crimes in which a gun is used. He proposed to end the sale of all military style rifles and to ban all handgun ownership by civilians unless they collect guns or target shoot, and they would have to justify their ownership of the weapons every five years. And finally, and considered to be the most controversial of Justice Minister Rocks proposals was the registration of all weapons ("Getting tough on guns," December 1, 1994).

On February 14, 1995, Justice Minister Rock unveiled Bill C-68, also called the Firearms Act. Gun proponents were adamantly against the Gun Registry as proposed by Justice Minister Rock. John Perocchio of the Canadian Firearms Action Council denounced the legislation by calling it "absolutely insane." He went on to state: "This is an unjust law and an unjust law is usually treated by society by being ignored." Wendy Cukier, leader of the Coalition for Gun Control, hoped that the justice minister would stick to his plan and enact the gun bill in its entirety. She stated: "There's no question the battle is far from over. We're expecting a tremendous backlash and we're hoping that the minister and the rest of the Liberal caucus will stand firm" (Campbell, February 15, 1995).

Even with the objections from gun groups, Bill C-68 was agreed on in principle on April 6, 1995. However, there was considerable dissent within the Liberal Party about the bill. Docherty (1997) found that MPs have a significant problem in Parliament when they have to weigh their home constituency against the desires of the party. Docherty found that when Bill C-68 was first being drafted; 30 Liberal MPs, mostly from rural ridings, voiced their opposition to the bill. When the bill was finally voted on to become law, there were still many Liberal MPs from rural ridings that were unsatisfied with the bill, and some broke ranks and voted against the bill. Those Liberals that broke rank were punished by

Prime Minister Jean Chretien and removed from committee appointments. However, Liberals from rural ridings faced a tough position with a conservative pro-gun constituency and a liberal pro-control government. The concern of these Liberal MPs is quite real when considering that the seats of MPs in Canada aren't nearly as safe as their counterpart in the United States and there is huge turnover each election.

Even with the dissent within the Liberal Party, Bill C-68 was given significant support. The entirety of the party Bloc Quebecois backed the passage of the bill (Ha, April 6, 1995). However, because of the criticism within the party, Justice Minister Rock decided that some provisions of the bill could be compromised on to gain the full support of the party, but he did not budge on the provision that called for the registration of all firearms ("Rock's gun control bill facing compromises," May 19, 1995).

On June 13, 1995, Bill C-68 was passed by the House of Commons. The bill also banned the future importation and sale of a wide variety of small and easily concealed handguns known as Saturday-night specials. The Liberals hoped to design the Gun Registry in a cost-effective way as well (Ha, June 14, 1995). On November 23, 1995 the Canadian Senate passed the gun bill as well. Justice Minister Rock stated: "We will now proceed to implement the system of registration in a way that's easy to use, practical and sensitive to the needs of recreational firearms community in this country. We'll need their (gun owners) assistance in achieving those goals." The Coalition for Gun Control was also impressed by the bill becoming law. Wendy Cukier of the Coalition for Gun Control stated: "It's going to be a while before we'll know what the impact is, but I'm confident that we've set a new course for the country" (Ha, November 23, 1995).

After the passage of Bill C-68, there was a considerable decrease in attention to gun control policy in Canada. However, the last of the major focusing events in Canada that this study focuses upon took place on September 27, 1996. Mark Chahal shot and killed his estranged wife and her entire family with his legally obtained firearms in Vernon, British Columbia. This event became known as the Vernon Massacre (Matas and Howard, September 28, 1996). However, besides a few comments about the incident by Minister Rock stating that Bill C-68 would help prevent these forms of disasters, there was no new gun control items placed on the agenda immediately after the event. This may have been due to the fact that Bill C-68 had just been recently passed and it took considerable will power by Justice Minister Rock, the Liberals, and gun control groups to get that piece of legislation passed. Also Bill C-68, the Firearms Act, had yet to be implemented, the majority of the provisions would not start being phased in for a few years. Thus, the legislation to prevent these types of events was on the books, even if they had yet to be implemented.

The next and final piece of gun control legislation that was passed by the Canadian Parliament was Bill C-15 in 2001. Bill C-15 was created in a way to modify and to fix Bill C-68. The reason that Bill C-15 was created was because of various design flaws with the Gun Registry. The changes made by Bill C-15 thus far appear to be just as ineffectual as the original Bill, C-68.

The last portion of this section goes into a discussion of the Gun Registry and its flaws. Brown-John (2003) examined the Gun Registry in order to understand where it had gone wrong. Brown-John found various issues that lead to the Gun Registry being widely regarded as inefficient. The first place that the Gun Registry had initially failed was allowing for provinces the right to opt out of doing registration, which is what the majority of western provinces did immediately. This forced the federal government to create institutions within the provinces to do the registration themselves. This cost the national government in Canada significantly.

Second the forms for registering firearms in Canada were extremely complicated and difficult for gun owners to fill out correctly. Over, 80% of all gun registration applications had errors on them and the gun owners had to personally sit with a member of the Gun Registry to correct paper work. This was an extremely costly activity. In order to rectify the problem forms were made more simple to use.

Third, the technology used for registering the firearms was designed poorly, was inefficient, and very costly. The technology that was used was supposed to cost in the neighborhood of 20% of the money budgeted to the Gun Registry. However, it has taken closer to 60% of the budget to maintain and operate the Gun Registry computer systems.

Fourth, the Gun Registry was a completely new government institution. Brown-John believed that with the creation of any new government there are inherent design problems. He likened the creation of the Gun Registry to the creation of the Office of Homeland Security in the United States. He argues that both are totally new institutions and with new institutions come many problems. Interestingly, both the Gun Registry and the Office of Homeland Security, which was created after the events of 9/11, were created in response to focusing events.

Finally, the Gun Registry is widely considered to be inefficient and a failure by Canadians because of the cost. When it was initially budgeted, it was thought that $85 million dollars would be enough to run the program. However, as of 2003, the Gun Registry had spent closer to $1 billion dollars (Brown-John 2003).

Analyzing the Major Canadian Themes

This final section evaluates the major themes about gun control policy and focusing events in Canada that were proposed in Chapter 2. The first major theme suggested that when there is a major focusing event and a left-of-center party or parties control policy making, there are often major overhauls to gun control policy. These left-of-center parties tend to work with the Coalition for Gun Control and are very reluctant to be influenced by pro-gun groups. Thus, in Canada, when there is a major focusing event, and leftist parties control government, gun control policy can be made relatively rapidly, efficiently, and the legislation created can lead to significant changes.

The second major theme suggests that when right-of-center parties control government in Canada, and major gun violence focusing events take place, gun control legislation can still be created. Right-of-center parties do appear to be more reluctant to create legislation; however, the pressure placed upon them by the Coalition for Gun Control and oftentimes by members of their party, in particular women (due to the feminist context to the gun control movement in Canada), has led to the Conservatives creating restrictive gun control laws after major focusing events. Thus, even when right-of-center parties control the policy-making process in Canada, restrictive gun control laws can still be made.

When we evaluate the first major theme, we find the data above provides strong support for it. The parliamentary government of Canada allowed the left-of-center parties the ability to dictate the type of restrictive legislation that would be placed upon the agenda. The Coalition for Gun Control, which was created after the Montreal Massacre, was able to provide considerable influence to politicians of all parties. However, when left-of-center parties were in control, the Coalition of Gun Control was far more influential than their opponents in the gun lobby. Thus, the perfect storm was created for a massive overhaul of the system, when a left-of-center party, the Liberals, was in control, and the presence of major focusing events, the Concordia shooting late in 1992 and the Georgina Leimonis murder right after the Liberals took over in 1993. These two events, coupled with the Liberals and their allies in the Coalition for Gun Control, laid the groundwork for a drastic overhaul to the gun control system, the creation of Bill C-68 and the Gun Registry. The Vernon Massacre is the one event that did not lead to new gun control legislation when it occurred; however, I argue that because it occurred so soon after the passage of Bill C-68, and the components of Bill C-68 had yet to be implemented the Liberals and the Coalition for

Gun Control used the event as a reaffirmation as to why the Gun Registry was created and not as a triggering event to create more legislation.

When we consider the second major theme of the Canadian section; we find significant support for it as well. The right-of-center party in power when the Montreal Massacre occurred, the Conservatives, did not initially have a strong desire to place gun control legislation on the agenda. In fact, Bill C-80, the first bill proposed after the event, died in committee. However, after its death there was considerable pressure by women from within the Conservative Party and from the group that would become the Coalition for Gun Control. This pressure trumped the lobbying efforts of the diffuse, multiheaded, multi-goaled and often unorganized gun lobby and led to the creation of Bill C-17. Bill C-17 was a watered-down version of Bill C-80 and did not appease the gun lobby nor did it appease gun control advocates. Sportsmen and gun enthusiasts believed the bill was punishing law-abiding citizens; whereas, gun control advocates considered the bill to be too weak. The data suggests that the Coalition for Gun Control, and its precursor, Canadians for Gun Control, were able to put enough pressure on the Conservative Party in power to create gun control legislation. However, because the Conservative Party is a right-of-center party, the ideology of its members helped water down Bill C-17 to make it less expansive than the bills that would later be created by Liberals.

Chapter 5

Conclusions: A Discussion of Why Canada Reacts to Gun Violence Events and the United States Does Not

Comparing Public Opinion in the United States vs Canada

When we consider Lipsets argument from earlier in the book, it could be assumed that the public opinion in Canada would strongly favor restrictive gun control legislation when compared to the United States. Unfortunately, the public opinion data that was available did not cover the full course of the study; however, the public opinion data that was used came at the height of the gun control movement in Canada. Because of this, the data that was available provides us with enough data to make accurate predictions on the differences and similarities between gun control opinion in the United States and Canada.

In 1996, the year of the Vernon Massacre in Canada and the creation of Bill C-68, it could be intuitively assumed that the public opinion in Canada would strongly support restrictive and comprehensive firearm controls. Unsurprisingly, 65% of the population of Canada did in fact favor Bill C-68 and the restraints created by it. Interestingly, when we look at the percentage of Americans who supported stricter gun control laws in a similar time period, 1995, we find that 62% of the population supported more restrictive gun control laws. This support in the United States was still high even after the creation of the Brady Bill and the Assault Weapons Ban, *and* the Republicans taking control of the House in 1994.

In 2002, Ipsos-Reid poll, the data showed that 53% of Canadians wanted to eliminate the Gun Registry and move away from the restrictive gun control laws created in the 1990s. In 2002, Gallup poll, 51% of the American public favored more restrictive gun control legislation. The data demonstrates that the Canadian public and the American public in 2002 had similar percentages of those who supported more gun control laws and those who supported less gun control laws. Likewise, in 2004, 52% of Canadians wanted to eliminate the Gun Registry; whereas, in the United States, 60% of the population favored more restrictive gun control legislation.

In 2006, when the Conservatives took control of the Parliament in Canada, 54% of the population wanted to eliminate the Gun Registry; however, 67% of the population believed in some form of gun registration. In 2006, 56% of the American public favored more restrictive gun control legislation.

In 2008, Angus Reid asked the Canadian public if they believed there should be a complete handgun ban. Only 45% of the Canadian public believed that there should be such a ban. When compared to a 2008 Gallup poll, only 29% of Americans were in favor of a complete ban on handguns.

The data compares some of the data taken from the case studies of the United States in Chapter 3 and Canada in Chapter 4. The public opinion data demonstrates that when compared; public attitudes on gun control policy in the United States and public attitudes on gun control policy in Canada, there was not a significant difference. The majority of both Canadians and Americans favored more restrictive gun control legislation. There appeared to be more Canadians favoring stricter gun control laws; however, this difference in attitudes does not appear to be considerably different.

In the United States gun control laws have historically been very lax and lenient at the national level. The major pieces of firearms legislation that were created in the late 1960s and the early 1990s have been insignificant in the long term. During the 1990s in Canada, there were several significant pieces of restrictive gun control legislation created. Yet, the public attitudes in the United States and Canada have not differed significantly from one another. Thus, does public attitudes on gun control in the two states matter significantly in determining policy outcomes?

It seems that Americans are less inclined to favor restrictive laws, and Canadians are more inclined to favor such laws; the difference in attitude is negligible enough that it is hard to rationalize that public opinion in either state is an overwhelming factor for why gun control laws differ. In fact, I would argue that the attitude of the public as a whole in both states has very little impact on the creation of new gun control laws. It is my belief that the segment of the population that is the most influential in policy making is interest groups. As Dahl (1956) stated, the minority interest group that has a strong and powerful stance that runs counter to a large apathetic majority will generally win in policy making. I believe that this is especially true in the United States, where the opinion of the NRA does not run in line with the majority of the public. This partially holds true in Canada, where the Coalition for Gun Control is more representative of the larger segments of the population, in particular the larger and more liberal eastern provinces. Thus, public opinion is an interesting point that must be discussed, but it is very hard to rationalize it being the primary, secondary, or even tertiary reason for why gun control policy differs between the United States and Canada.

Comparing the Influence of Government Structure and Party Influence: A Review of Agenda Setting and Formulation in Both the United States and Canada

When we review the agenda attention and formulation data from the case studies of the United States and Canada, we find that there is a significant difference in the number of gun bills proposed by Congress and by Parliament. The United States has proposed hundreds of gun control bills over the course of the study, but only a few have become law. In Canada, only a few gun control bills have been proposed, but the majority of them have become law. The reason for the stark contrast in bill proposals is due to the structure of government in the United States when compared to Canada. Bills have little chance of becoming law in the US presidential system; however, in Canada, when a bill is proposed by the government it has a very strong likelihood of becoming law.

Interestingly, even though the United States has proposed hundreds of bills and Canada just a few, the number of federal laws that have been created in both countries from 1963 to 2008 are similar. There have been six federal laws created in the United States, and five federal laws created in Canada. However, where we see a major difference is that three of the six federal laws created by the United States were lenient in nature; whereas, all the laws created in Canada were restrictive.

The data suggests that the United States proposes so many gun control bills because they so rarely make it past the agenda-setting stage. In Canada, gun control legislation is proposed rarely, but when it is proposed it nearly always becomes law, especially if the gun control legislation is restrictive in nature. Thus, the structure of government is very influential in determining the success of a proposed gun control bill. In the United States the bill is expected to die, and in Canada the bill is expected to become law.

Now, I turn to investigate the importance of parties in both countries. I argued in my major themes in Chapter 2 that the party in power would influence agenda attention and formulation, when coupled with a major focusing event. Surprisingly, in Chapter 3, even when Republicans were in control of the government, there were a significant number of restrictive gun control bills being proposed. However, the only time that restrictive gun control policy was created and formulated was when there was a unified Democrat government. Thus, the party in power may not be able to dictate agenda attention to gun control, but it can dictate whether gun control legislation will be formulated in the United States.

In Canada, I also argued that the party in power would be able to dictate what type of legislation would be created after a major focusing event. When right-of-center parties were in power, they were unable to prevent the restrictive gun control bill from moving to the formulation stage. This was widely due to the pressure placed upon the Conservative Party by the Coalition for Gun Control and from women within the party. When left-of-center parties were in control of government, restrictive gun control legislation was placed on the agenda and then formulated and implemented. Thus, right-of-center parties have a difficult time keeping restrictive gun control legislation off the agenda and from being formulated because of pressure from factions within the party and from a powerful pro-gun control lobby; whereas, left-of-center parties are able to formulate restrictive gun control legislation after a major focusing event because of support from a powerful pro-gun control lobby.

Comparing Interest Groups: The National Rifle Association vs the Coalition for Gun Control

In the United States, the NRA is the key group in determining the success and failure of proposed gun control legislation. The NRA is an adamant and steadfast pro-gun group that has no desire to allow proposed restrictive gun control legislation the light of day. In Canada, the Coalition for Gun Control is the ultimate actor in influencing the success and failure of proposed gun control legislation. Unlike the NRA, the Coalition for Gun Control is a rather new group, less than 20 years old, but its power in influencing the creation of new restrictive gun control is unquestioned.

Each of these two groups has come to dominant gun control policy in their respective country. Why?

Though the NRA and the Coalition for Gun Control share entirely different viewpoints on the gun control issue, they both have a single-minded resolve that is uncompromising to their opponents. They both have effective lobbyists and spokespersons that are able to influence policy makers. They each have powerful leaders that are able to organize their group in a way to make it efficient in its goals. And with the NRA, and likely the Coalition for Gun Control, they outspend their opposition by huge margins.

The opposition groups in both countries are far less powerful. In the United States, the Brady Campaign took years to organize properly and has yet to gain the influence in Washington like the NRA. The Brady Campaign also has the disadvantage of less money and of employing fewer lobbyists than the NRA. The NFA is one of many gun lobbyists groups in Canada; however, as stated in Chapter 4, the gun groups of Canada have a significant problem organizing and banding together to express a single goal. This lack of cohesion has prevented pro-gun groups from acting as a single and powerful actor to influence Canadian policy makers. Thus in regards to pro-gun groups in Canada, the united stand, and the divided fall.

The power of the dominant interest groups in each country is significant. The NRA has been able to maintain its stranglehold on policy creation because of various reasons. First, the NRA is well organized and well-funded by its members and by gun manufacturers. The budget of the NRA dwarfs its competition in the Brady Campaign. This allows for the NRA the ability to hire more lobbyists who pursue the NRA's goals vigorously in Congress. Along with the ability to influence politicians directly, the NRA is able to influence politicians because of their campaign tactics.

After the gun control legislation was created in 1992 and 1993, the NRA responded by attacking many Democrats who had supported the Brady Bill and the Assault Weapons Ban. The NRA did not just attack these politicians with campaign ads on gun control; they ran ads on issues that did not pertain to gun control as a means to undermine that Congressional member. In 1994, the NRA spent more on elections than any other interest group. The ability to spend, and spend big in a variety of ways to undermine gun control opposition is a prime reason why the NRA is so powerful and so very frightening to gun control proponents (Dreyfuss 1995).

Second, the NRA has an intense membership base. As Dahl (1956) argued, intense minorities when dealing with a generally apathetic majority allows for minority tyranny of the majority. With the NRA, this is exactly the case. The NRA has been able to have significant sway over policy creation because of the intensity of it and its members. Thus, policy creation in the United States tends to mirror the views of this small intense minority, rather than reflect the attitudes of the general public.

The Coalition for Gun Control was born out of the Montreal Massacre. They were a loose coalition of people, mainly women, who were outraged about the slayings and wanted there to be change. The Coalition for Gun Control initially was more of a political movement than an organized interest group; however, this group quickly gained in influence with the public and with Parliament. The pressure that they placed on the Parliament eventually led to the creation of restrictive gun control policy. As time progressed, the Coalition for Gun Control became a formalized and influential group. I argue that two primary factors have led to the Coalition for Gun Control's rise in influence and power. First, the large amount of public support for the Coalition for gun Control and its goals convinced Canadian politician that it had to act. Second, the Coalition is single minded in its support of the regulation, restriction, or removal of all firearms. This unification of purpose in a single powerful interest group has allowed for it to be more influential than the weaker and more fragmented pro-gun interest groups in Canada.

When we consider interest groups and their influence in policy creation after a focusing event, we can view the NRA as a group that is able to retard the impact of an event and help prevent legislation from being created by either major political party in the United States. In Canada, the Coalition for Gun Control has been very influential in motivating policy makers from both parties to create gun control legislation after a focusing event. Thus, it can be argued that interest group influence is one of the primary reasons that gun control legislation is either created or prevented after a major focusing event.

The Final Discussion: An Evaluation of the Major Theme of the Book

Like Pal (2003), I found that the role of institutions and interest groups is particularly important in determining the outcome of policy. Like Pal (2003), and Mauser and Margolis (1992), I also found that the role of public opinion and culture were not influential enough in determining the differences in gun control policy in the United States and Canada. My study adds a bit more spice to the pot because it brings in a discussion of parties and most importantly a more in-depth discussion of the importance of focusing events. Pal (2003) briefly mentions that events appear to cause policy activity, but does not take in an in-depth study of them.

When the data from the entire book is analyzed, we find that the major theme of the book holds true: the United States is less responsive to major focusing events than Canada in all ways but one. The United States proposes more gun control legislation than Canada every Congressional term; however, gun control legislation rarely leaves the agenda-setting stage, much less move forward to the formulation stage. Thus, I believe that the United States is more responsive at the agenda-setting level; however, the data shows that gun control legislation is nearly never created in the United States, even after major focusing events. This means that from the formulation stage to the implementation stage the United States is far less responsive than Canada.

Throughout the book I have discussed the key factors that may influence policy making. These key factors are: culture, public attitudes, governmental institutions, interest groups, and political parties. Earlier in the book, I argued that culture and public attitudes are less important in determining policy outcomes than governmental institutions, interest groups, and parties. At this juncture in the book, I believe that it is important to discuss which factors are the most important in determining gun control policy after a major focusing event. It is my belief, of all the factors discussed interest groups are the most important.

Interest groups, as demonstrated in discussion and from the *New York Times* and the *Globe and Mail* are quite capable of determining whether or not a bill will become law because of their ability to sway politicians. In the United States, the NRA makes it virtually impossible for federal gun control legislation to be created; generally Republicans share the NRA's view on gun control, and generally Democrats fear the same sort of backlash that they faced in 1994. In Canada, the Coalition for Gun Control was able to twist the arm of the Conservative Party to create gun control legislation after the Montreal Massacre. The Coalition for Gun Control has also had significant pull in determining the severity of the gun control legislation that was created thereafter in Canada.

In my opinion, the second most important factor is the institutional arrangement of government. When a bill is proposed in the US Congress, its chance of becoming law is slim. However, in Canada when a government bill is proposed the chance of it becoming law is very good. As discussed earlier, gun control bills are proposed in every Congressional session, but these bills rarely become law. Even when there is the presence of a major focusing event, the likelihood of one of the proposed bills becoming law is very slim. Thus, focusing events in the United States have the ability to increase the number of gun bills placed on the agenda, but have very little impact on moving the bill to the formulation stage.

In Canada, gun control legislation is almost never proposed. However, when there are major focusing events in Canada, gun control legislation is often proposed. Because of the design of parliamentary government, government bills usually become law. Thus, focusing events in Canada are very important because not only do they lead to more gun control laws being placed on the Canadian agenda, but because of the form of government, these laws are generally formulated and implemented as well.

Finally, the third most important factor is the party in power. In the United States when the Republicans control government, or when there is divided government, restrictive gun control legislation has never been created. The only time restrictive gun control legislation has ever been created was when the Democrats had unified control of government. In Canada, the only time a right-of-center party has ever proposed restrictive gun control legislation was after the Montreal Massacre and this was due to pressure from interest groups and from pressure within the party itself. The bill that was created was very weak in the opinion of gun control groups. The story is quite different when left-of-center parties control Parliament. The largest and most comprehensive piece of gun control that was created, the Gun Registry, was created when there was control of government by left-of-center parties in Canada. In fact, when left-of-center parties have controlled Canadian government, there has never been a piece of lenient gun control proposed.

It is my belief that this book has demonstrated the significance of focusing events in influencing gun control policy in both the United States and Canada. In both countries focusing events impact agenda setting. In the United States, bill proposals increase after major events, and when no events are present, lenient bill proponents become active. In Canada, it takes a major focusing event before gun control policy is placed upon the agenda. However, the shock of a focusing event is not enough to drive a bill into creation. Other significant factors come in to play. Thus, focusing events impact bill proposals at the agenda-setting stage, but the role of interest groups, government institutions, and political parties determines whether the bill will be formulated and implemented.

Chapter 6

Gun Control Policy in the United States and Canada: 2008 to Present

This book has discussed how the United States and Canada have responded to major gun violence events. Chapter 6 provides an overview of the changes in gun control policy in the United States and Canada from 2008 until the present.

United States: Public Attitudes on Firearms

In Chapter 3, it was demonstrated that gun control policy has often been favored by a majority of the American public, but this view has not translated into gun control policy at the national level. The gun control polls that are discussed below were accumulated by *PollingReport.com*.

As seen in earlier polls, the public between 2008 and present have often sought stronger controls on firearms. For example, a June 6, 2011 *Time* poll found that 51% of the public favored stricter gun control, 7% favored less strict gun laws, and 39% thought gun laws were about right. A CBS News/*New York Times Poll* found that 46% of the public wanted stricter laws, 13% less strict, and 38% wanted the bills to be left the same. The poll also demonstrated that in the general public there is a drastic difference in opinion when political party is taken in to consideration. For example, only 27% of Republicans thought gun laws should be made stricter as opposed to 68% of Democrats polled.

The two aforementioned polls demonstrate that the public opinion on gun control policy is split. Many favor stricter gun control laws, yet many feel that the laws are acceptable as they are or should be made more lenient. The polls that have been conducted since 2008 also demonstrate that there is a partisan tilt on gun control opinion. This tilt, though inferred in early chapters, is clearly demonstrated in these latter polls.

However, with all of this in mind, we must still understand that the public's opinion on gun control appears to have very little impact on gun control policy in the United States. Though it is interesting to understand how the public views firearms, the public's attitude on firearms is not a good measure to determine whether gun control policy will be created.

An Overview of Congress and the Presidency

In November of 2008, Senator Barack Obama a Democrat from Illinois defeated Senator John McCain a Republican from Arizona for the US Presidency. Not only did Senator Obama win the Presidency, but his party, the Democrats, won majority control in both the US House of Representatives and the US Senate.

This election was the first time that the Democrats had gained control of the Presidency and both chambers of Congress since the debacle that was the 1994 election. In 1994, gun control policy was a significant reason why the Democrats lost the House; however, history is prone to repeat itself. Based on the discussion from previous chapters, it could be assumed that with the political environment set the way that it was, gun control policy could once again be placed on the policy agenda.

On November 5, 2009 Nidal Malik Hasan shot and killed 13 people and wounded 29 others at Fort Hood in Texas. This was a major focusing event that took place with unified Democrat control of government. Unfortunately, this event was not the last major focusing event to take place since 2008.

On January 8, 2011, Representative Gabrielle Gifford's, a three-term Congressional member from Arizona was wounded in an assassination attempt. During the course of the shooting, six people were killed including US District Judge John Roll. This event coupled with the mass murder that took place in November of 2009 might lead us to believe gun control policy would be created. However, in November of 2010, the Republicans recaptured the House of Representatives. With divided government and other factors, it appeared unlikely that new gun control legislation would be created, even after these two horrific events.

In order to test Congressional agenda attention to gun control policy, I once again turned to the electronic version of the Congressional Index found on *Thomas.gov*. As I used in Chapter 3, all bills that targeted constraints and bans on firearms or ammunition were included as restrictive bills. Legislation that was introduced to make the ownership of firearms easier was included as lenient bills.

The 111th Congress, 2009–10, found the Democrats in control of both branches of Congress for the first time since 1994. With this retaking of Congress and the major focusing event that took place at Fort Hood Texas, it might be assumed that gun control policy would once again be a major political issue on the Congressional agenda. However, even with unified Democrat control of the government, agenda attention to gun control policy has been low.

In the US House of Representatives, there were seven pieces of restrictive legislation proposed. The majority of the legislation appeared to seek incremental changes in gun control policy. Some examples of restrictive gun control policy were: preventing loop holes in gun sales at gun shows, and to prevent access to guns to children. None of the bills proposed in the House appeared to be in direct response to the mass murder at Fort Hood.

Meanwhile, there were 20 lenient gun bills proposed. Unlike the restrictive bill proposals, some of the lenient bill proposals appeared to be rather significant in their goals. Two examples of more expansive legislation were: to make the interstate sale of firearms much easier, and to prevent any form of national data base in registering or recording the sale of firearms. Some of the other bills included: the ability to make it easier for collectors to obtain firearms, to prevent military personnel from having to register their privately owned firearms, and to have more freedom in carrying firearms on federal land.

When we review the bills that were proposed in the 111th Congress, we might be surprised that gun control policy was not a very salient issue. With the presence of a major focusing event, and unified control of government by the Democrats, it is peculiar that a stronger push for more firearms controls wasn't sought. However, lenient bill proponents appeared to be unfazed by Democrat control, and a large number of these bills were proposed.

In the US Senate, there were five pieces of restrictive legislation proposed. All of the restrictive bills appeared to be relatively modest in their proposals. The most restrictive piece of legislation that was proposed wanted to tighten background checks at gun shows. Other restrictive bill proposals sought to prevent the carrying of firearms on trains, and airplanes. The one piece of legislation that was proposed seemingly in response to the Fort Hood slayings was designed to make federal facilities more secure. This proposed legislation sought to make federal buildings and locations safe not only to the people that work there, but to people who may be visiting the facility. None of the restrictive bills that were proposed made it out of committee.

At the same time in the Senate, there were eleven pieces of lenient gun control legislation proposed. For the most part, I would argue that the majority of the lenient bills proposed sought modest changes as well. Two focused on making it easier for gun collectors to obtain antiquated firearms. One sought reciprocity in concealed carry laws. Some of the bills appeared to be proposed as a direct counter to restrictive bill proposals. For example, one bill sought to allow people the right to carry firearms on trains and another sought to protect military personnel from having to register their privately owned firearms, which appears to be directly counter to making federal facilities safer. Of the lenient bills that were proposed none of them became law.

Like in the House of Representatives, I am somewhat surprised that gun control policy was not a more salient issue when there was unified Democrat control and the presence of a major focusing event. Yet, restrictive gun control policy appears to have barely touched upon the consciousness of policy makers. In regards to overall bill proposals, it seems that lenient gun bill proponents were more active in pursuing lenient gun control policy than those seeking restrictive.

I believe that the reason for this lack of attention in the 111th Congress stems from two factors. First, I would argue that Democrats were still very concerned to tackle the gun control issue after the major defeat the party took in 1994. I think that gun control policy for the most part is a taboo issue to Democrats, it generally will not help a policy maker win an election, and it could very well be the reason that they are defeated by a challenger. Second, the push by President Obama and the Democrats to create a national health care policy took significant political capital. Had the Democrats been pushing for a national health care policy, *and* more restrictive gun control policy, in my opinion, the back lash would have been overwhelming.

In November of 2010, the Republicans once again captured the US House of Representatives. The Democrats were able to maintain control of the Senate, but they did lose seats. Unlike in 1994, the Democrats did not lose the House because of gun control issues, but rather due to backlash from other issues. Nonetheless, the 112th Congress of the United States marked the end of unified government for the Democrats, and once again marked a time of divided government.

On January 8, 2011, a serving member of the US House of Representatives, Gabrielle Giffords, was nearly assassinated by a deranged gun man. Due to the fact that Giffords was a member of the House of Representatives, it might be assumed that the House would react to this focusing event. In fact, the House of Representatives proposed two pieces of restrictive gun control legislation that dealt specifically with this event.

The first of these bills was House Bill 361, also known as the Freedom to Serve Without Fear Act, which would prevent the carrying of firearms on or near federal property, especially when a member of the federal government was on premises. House Bill 496, the Protection of Federal Events Act, would prevent individuals from carrying firearms on or near federal buildings when a federal official was in a building for campaigning or handling official representational issues. Neither of these bills has made it from committee as of yet.

Along with the two bills that were proposed as direct response to the Giffords shooting, the House proposed five other pieces of restrictive legislation. These bills had modest goals such as: tightening up background checks at gun shows.

Meanwhile, there have been eight lenient gun bills proposed in the 112th Congress. None of the bills proposed thus far have sought vast or sweeping changes to federal gun policy. Examples of the lenient bills that have been proposed are: reciprocity from states in carrying concealed weapons and to create legislation to protect gun collectors.

In all of the 111th Congress, there were only seven restrictive gun bills proposed; however, in the 112th Congress which is controlled by the Republicans, there have already been seven restrictive bills proposed. I believe that the Giffords attempted assassination has had a larger impact on House members than did the Fort Hood slayings. The impact of this event is larger because Giffords is a member of the House, and this attempted assassination has made many House members feel as if they could be a victim of such a crime. Due to the event, gun control policy is more in the consciousness of policy makers, and this has led to more restrictive bill proposals and for bill proposals that will potentially help protect the federal officials themselves.

In the Senate of the 112th Congress, there have been four restrictive bills proposed and four lenient bills proposed. In the US House, there were two bills proposed that would make federal facilities more secure for federal officials when they were there in some official capacity. However, in the Senate, up to this point, there has been no such bill proposed.

The restrictive bills proposed so far in the Senate have been modest in their goals, such as more background checks at gun shows.

Two of the lenient bills proposed in the Senate have been moderate in their goals: reciprocity between states on concealed carry and the protection of gun collectors. Both of these bills appear to favor incremental change. However, one of the bills proposed appears to be seeking larger amounts of change. This bill wants to prevent any form of cataloging firearm sales and to prevent any form of Gun Registry.

As of yet, the bills proposed in both the House and in the Senate have had gained very little footing. The Fort Hood shooting, appeared to have limited impact on gun agenda attention; however, the attempted assassination of Gabrielle Giffords on the other hand appears to have led to increased agenda attention, especially in the House. However, even with the presence of these two major focusing events, I predict that new restrictive gun control policy will not be created. I make this prediction based on history. Never has a piece of restrictive federal legislation been created when the Republicans control at least one chamber of Congress. And for this reason, I cannot imagine restrictive gun control legislation will be created in the near future.

The US Supreme Court: Groundbreaking Decisions on Gun Policy

Throughout the first five chapters, I barely made mention of the Second Amendment of the US Constitution. The reason for this was simple, besides being used as rhetoric by the NRA, the Second Amendment of the Constitution was rarely cited by policy makers. In fact, before 2008, when the Supreme Court of the United States ruled on the Second Amendment, its interpretation was counter to the NRA's argument that the Second Amendment provided the individual right to own a firearm. However, in 2008, *District of Columbia v. Heller,* and once again in 2010, *McDonald v. Chicago*, the US Supreme Court in two groundbreaking decisions changed that. The following briefly discusses the long-standing precedent held on the Second Amendment by the US Supreme Court, and the more recent changes that have come about due to the aforementioned cases.

The Second Amendment of the Constitution states: "A well-regulated militia, being necessary to the security of a free state, the right of the people to keep and bear arms, shall not be infringed." The NRA has long cited the Second Amendment as the main reason that gun control policy that limits the ownership of firearms should be prohibited. However, before 2008, this argument by the NRA was thwarted by long-existing precedent. In 1876 the Court ruled in *U.S v. Cruikshank (1876)* "that (the right to bear arms) is not a right granted by the Constitution. Neither is it in any manner an instrument for its existence. The Amendment says it's not to be infringed upon, but this means simply that it is not to be infringed on by the Congress." In the case *Presser v. Illinois (1886)* the court ruled that the Second Amendment did not apply to states, and that the Second Amendment only pertained to national laws. States had the right to make their own gun policy in their own way. Also in Texas a law was passed that it was illegal to carry dangerous weapons, which included firearms. This law was challenged by the case *Miller v. Texas (1894)* which upheld the state law, and dismissed the challenge by Miller. Thus, before 2008, the US Court deemed the Second Amendment as not being an individual right and that it did not apply to the states.

However, in 2008, the US Supreme Court provided a new interpretation of the Second Amendment. *District of Columbia v. Heller (2008)* found that it was constitutional for individuals to own firearms for legal purposes such as self-defense. This case was a landmark decision because it was the first time that the US Supreme Court found that the possession of firearms was an individual right. Likewise, the 2010 case of *McDonald v. Chicago (2010),* found that the Second Amendment applied to the states and must be incorporated by using the Due Process Clause of the Fourteenth Amendment. Since 2008, the US Supreme Court has ruled that not only is the Second Amendment an individual right, but the Second Amendment also applies to the states.

I realize that the above discussion falls somewhat outside of the scope of my book. However, these two major decisions by the Supreme Court impact gun control policy as much, if not more, than any piece of legislation that has been crafted by Congress. The US Supreme Court has potentially prevented states and local government from making gun control policy. Because of these decisions the way in which the federal government handles gun control policy becomes all the more important. No longer can gun control proponents rely on the states to make the restrictive policy that they have often sought. Thus, these two court cases dramatically change the dynamics of gun control policy making at all levels of the process and make the study of federal gun control policy making even more important.

Canada: An Overview from 2008 until the Present

Since 2006, the Conservative Party of Canada has held a majority in Canadian Parliament. Though there have been no major focusing events, the Gun Registry that was created in response to a number of major focusing events in the 1990s, has been under serious attack by Conservatives. This section updates the current state of the Gun Registry in Canada and analyzes how the public, policy makers, and interest groups view the Gun Registry and the potential changes that may be made to it.

Prior to 2008, lenient gun bill proposals were nearly nonexistent. However, since 2008, the Conservative Party in Canada has proposed a series of new firearms bills, and all of them have attempted to rework the Firearms Registry, or to repeal the Gun Registry. In October of 2007, Bill C-24 was proposed. The bill wanted to eliminate the provision of the Firearms Registry that required nonrestricted firearms to be registered. This bill made it to First Reading, where it was eventually defeated. However, the Conservative Party was not discouraged and two important private members bills were proposed: C-301 and C-391 (www.parl.gc.ca/LegisInfo/BillDetails).

Bill C-301 was a private member bill proposed by MP Garry Breitkreuz on February 9, 2009. His bill would have ended the registration of rifles and shotguns, as well as softening controls on machine guns, by allowing people to transport fully automatic and semiautomatic assault guns to public shooting ranges (CBC News). His bill met stiff opposition from the Coalition for Gun Control. President Wendy Cukier stated that the bill would effectively dismantle gun control policy in Canada. Another detractor for the bill, the Canadian Associations of Chiefs of Police, stated: "All guns are potentially dangerous. All gun owners need to be licensed. All guns need to be registered and gun owners need to be accountable for their firearms. We oppose Bill C-301 as a retrogressive proposal that cannot, in any way, benefit the safety and security of Canadians" (CBC News). Bill C-301 ultimately was defeated on June 15, 2009 (www.parl.gc.ca/LegisInfo/BillDetails). However, his bill would not be the last bill proposed by the Conservatives in 2009.

Bill C-391 was proposed by MP Candice Hoeppner in May of 2009. The bills goal was to eliminate provisions of the Gun Registry that would require individuals to register unrestricted firearms such as rifles and shotguns. The bill made it to Second Reading; however, it was defeated there by a vote of (153–151) on September 22, 2010. The Coalition for Gun Control along with other groups advocated strongly against this bill becoming law. Bill C-391 demonstrates that the Coalition for Gun Control is a very powerful and influential group in policy making (www.parl.gc.ca/LegisInfo/BillDetails).

The previous discussion outlines how the Conservatives have tried to repeal the Gun Registry. Their attempt to repeal major portions of it with Bill C-391 was nearly successful. It took the strong efforts of the Coalition for Gun Control and other groups to prevent the bill from becoming law. With the Conservatives' multiple attempts to repeal the Gun Registry, we may believe that not only are the Conservatives desirous of a repeal of the Gun Registry but so too are the Canadian people. The next discussion demonstrates that this is not necessarily the case.

An Ipsos-Reid poll that was conducted from September to October of 2010 for Postmedia News and Global Television found that public attitudes on the Gun Registry aren't as negative as the Conservatives are portraying. The Gun Registry has overwhelming support in most Canadian provinces: 81% of the residents of Quebec, 66% of the residents of Ontario, 61% of the residents of British Columbia, 57% of the residents of Saskatchewan and Manitoba, and 59% of the residents of the Atlantic Provinces. The only province that had a majority of its citizens oppose the Gun Registry was Alberta, with 53% of the population favoring a repeal of the Gun Registry (Kennedy, October 5, 2010). This poll demonstrates that the push by the Conservatives to eliminate the Gun Registry may not be because of public pressures but more for political motivations.

Final Discussion

The information in this chapter has updated the state of gun control policy up to July, 2011. In the United States there were two major focusing events that were identified and discussed. However, new gun control legislation was not created and it appears unlikely that new gun control legislation will be created.

Meanwhile in Canada, the Gun Registry has become a hot topic to the Conservative government that currently controls Parliament. However, the public, anti-firearm interest groups, and left-of-center parties all appear to favor the continuation of the Gun Registry. In my opinion if the Conservatives would in fact repeal the Gun Registry, with the number of entities opposing them, it may be a huge political hit to them and could lead to a loss of power. For this reason, it may be unlikely that the Conservatives will repeal the Gun Registry.

Bibliography

ABC News/*Washington Post* Poll, "Do you favor or oppose stricter gun control laws for this country?" 1999–2009.

—, "Would you oppose or support a ban on the sale of all assault weapons?" 1999.

—, "Would the public favor a ban on assault weapons?" 2007.

Angus-Reid Poll, "Would a countrywide ban on handguns be effective in lowering crime?" 2008.

Archer, Keith; Gibbins, Roger; Knopff, Rainer; Pal, Leslie A., *Parameters of Power: Canada's Political Institutions*. Scarborough, ON: ITP Nelson International Thomson Publishing Company, 1999.

Associated Press, "Gun Lobby Criticizes President on Assault-Weapons Proposals," *New York Times* (1857–current file), New York, NY: May 2, 1994, p. A14.

—, "Head of Rifle Group Calls Dr. King's Death 'Senseless,'" *New York Times* (1857–current file), New York, NY: April 12, 1968, p. 20.

—, "President Appeals for Gun Controls," *New York Times* (1857–current file), New York, NY: May 10, 1968, p. 40.

—, "Reagan Signs Measure Relaxing Gun Controls," *New York Times* (1857–current file), New York, NY: May 20, 1986, p. A16.

—, "Rifle Group's Aide Doubtful on Effect of Gun Curb Bills," *New York Times* (1857–current file), New York, NY: June 6, 1968, p. 22.

—, "Tydings Scores Rifle Group," *New York Times* (1857–current file), New York, NY: June 10, 1968, p. 29.

Baumgartner, Frank R. and Bryan D. Jones, *Agendas and Instability in American Politics*. Chicago: University of Chicago Press, 1993.

Birkland, Thomas, *After Disaster: Agenda-Setting, Public Policy, and Focusing Events*. Washington: Georgetown University Press, 1997.

—, *Lessons of Disaster: Policy Change After Catastrophic Events*. Washington, DC: Georgetown University Press, 2006.

Boyd, Gerald M., "Bush Opposes a Ban on Assault Firearms but Backs State Role," *New York Times* (1857–current file), New York, NY: February 17, 1989.

Brown-John, Lloyd C., "Assessing the Canada Firearms Registration System: Hey It Was Only A Billion Dollars." Presented at 2003 ACSUS Conference, Portland OR, November 19–23.

Bruni, Frank, "Gun Control Bill Rejected in House in Bipartisan Vote," *New York Times* (1857–current file), New York, NY: June 19, 1999, p. A1.

—, "Lott Warns He May Shelve Bill With Gun Restrictions," *New York Times* (1857–current file), New York, NY: May 18, 1999, p. A18.

—, "Senate Will Debate Gun Control Issues," *New York Times* (1857–current file), New York, NY: May 7, 1999, p. A1.

Burnham, David, "Measure to Relax Gun Rules Denounced by Police Groups," *New York Times* (1857–current file), New York, NY: January 31, 1986, p. B8.

Campbell, Murray, "Justice Minister sticks to his guns on registration, legislation faces tough road as Rock makes just one concession," *Globe and Mail*, Toronto, Canada: February 15, 1995.

CBC News, "New federal bill would end long gun registry," CBC News. April 1, 2009.

CBS News/*New York Times* Poll, "Do you favor or oppose the nationwide ban on assault weapons?" 2000.

—, "In general, do you think gun control laws should be made more strict, less strict or kept as they are now?" January 15–19, 2011.

Clerous, Richard and Craig McInnes, "Aftermath in Montreal: Opposition MPs demand long-promised gun control amendment," *Globe and Mail*, Toronto, Canada: December 8, 1989.

Cobb, Roger W. and Charles D. Elder, *Participation in American Politics: The Dynamics of Agenda-Building* (2nd edn). Baltimore: Johns Hopkins University Press.

Cobb, Roger W. and Marc Howard Ross (eds), *Cultural Strategies of Agenda Denial*. Lawrence, KS: Kansas University Press, 1997.

Cobb, Roger W., Jeannie Keith-Ross, and Marc Howard Ross, "Agenda Building as Comparative Political Process," *American Political Science Review* 70: 126–38, 1976.

Cohen, Michael, James March, and Johan Olsen, "A Garbage Can Model of Organizational Choice," *Administrative Science Quarterly* 17: 1–25, March, 1972.

Dahl, Robert, *A Preface to Democratic Theory*. Chicago: The University of Chicago Press, 1956.

Davidson, Osha Gray, *Under Fire: The NRA and the Battle for Gun Control*. New York: Henry Holt & Company, 1993.

Delacourt, Susan, "Gun control divides Tory women," *Globe and Mail*, Toronto, Canada: February 8, 1991.

—, "Ottawa ponders gun ban in cities, Rock promises tighter laws on firearms and young offenders," *Globe and Mail*, Toronto, Canada: April 12, 1994.

Docherty, David C., *Mr. Smith Goes to Ottawa: Life in the House of Commons*. Vancouver, BC: University of British Columbia Press, 1997.

Dowd, Maureen, "Under Siege, N.R.A. Fights 'The Hysteria,'" *New York Times* (1857–current file), New York, NY: March 18, 1989, p. 1.

Downs, Anthony, "Up and Down with Ecology: The Issue Attention Cycle," *Public Interest* 28: 38–50, 1972.

Dreyfuss, Robert, "Political Snipers," *The American Prospect*. September 15, 1995.

Dye, Thomas, *Understanding Public Policy* (11th edn). Upper Saddle River, NJ: Pearson Prentice Hall. Copyright 2005.

Eaton, Leslie and Michael Luo, "Shooting Rekindles Issues of Gun Rights and Restrictions," *New York Times*, New York, NY: April 18, 2007, p. 20.

Eckholm, Erik, "A Little Gun Control, A Lot of Guns," *New York Times* (1857–current file), New York, NY: August 15, 1993, p. E1.

Erikson, Robert S., Michael B. Mackuen, and James A. Stimson, *The Macro Polity.* Cambridge: Cambridge University Press, 2002.

Finney, John W., "Congress Leaders Call Stricter Gun Law Unlikely," *New York Times* (1857–current file), New York, NY: June 8, 1968, p. 27.

—, "Gun Control Bill Blocked in House," *New York Times* (1857–current File), New York, NY: June 11, 1968, p. 1.

—, "Gun Control Bill Passed in Senate," *New York Times* (1857–current file), New York, NY: September 19, 1968, p. 1.

—, "Gun Control Bill Speeded by House, Passage Scheduled Today for Anticrime Measure," *New York Times* (1857–current file), New York, NY: June 6, 1968, p. 23.

—, "Rifle Group Mounts Drive Against Gun Controls," *New York Times* (1857–current file), New York, NY: June 15, 1968, p. 1.

—, "Senate Approves Pistol Sales Curb, But Wont Ban Mail Order Purchase of Rifles," *New York Times* (1857–current file), New York, NY: May 17, 1968, p. 36.

—, "Senate Chiefs Call for Caution on Johnson Gun Control Plans," *New York Times* (1857–current file), New York, NY: June 10, 1968, p. 1.

—, "Senators Predict Strict Gun Curbs As Pressure Rises," *New York Times* (1857–current file), New York, NY: June 13, 1968, p. 1.

—, "Strong Gun Curbs Pressed by Clark," *New York Times* (1857–current file), New York, NY: September 11, 1968, p. 19.

Frankel, Max, "Johnson Asks Strong Gun Law," *New York Times* (1857–current file), New York, NY: June 7, 1968, p. 1.

—, "President Calls for Registering of All Firearms," *New York Times* (1857–current file), New York, NY: June 25, 1968, p. 1.

Franklin, Ben A., "Gun Problem; The Citizens Arm As Congress Looks the Other Way," *New York Times* (1857–current file), New York, NY: April 21, 1968, p. E3.

Fraser, Graham, "Aftermath in Montreal: Lewis willing to look at need for safety course in gun law amendments," *Globe and Mail,* Toronto, Canada: December 9, 1989.

—, "Gun bill 'uniquely Canadian,' country has 'own firearm culture,' Campbell says," *Globe and Mail,* Toronto, Canada: November 7, 1991.

—, "Rural and urban opinions differ sharply over federal bill to limit gun control legislation," *Globe and Mail,* Toronto, Canada: December 7, 1990.

Gallup Poll, "Do you feel that the laws covering the sale of firearms should be made more strict, less strict, or kept as they are now?" 1999–2008.

—, "Do you think there should or should not be a law that would ban the possession of handguns, except by the police and other authorized persons?" 1959–2008.

—, "Would the public favor the registration of all handguns?" 1985–2000.

Gibbon, Ann and Andre Picard, "Two die in campus rampage, Montreal professor to be charged in Concordia shooting spree," *Globe and Mail,* Toronto, Canada: August 25, 1992.

Globe and Mail, "Aftermath in Montreal: Ease of getting gun in Canada 'unacceptable,' Mulroney says," *Globe and Mail,* Toronto, Canada: December 11, 1989.

—, "Election 1993: What the parties promise," *Globe and Mail,* Toronto, Canada: October 5, 1993.

—, "Getting tough on guns," *Globe and Mail,* Toronto, Canada: December 1, 1994.

—, "New year to bring battery of gun safety regulations," *Globe and Mail,* Toronto, Canada: December 31, 1993.

—, "Rock's gun control bill facing compromises," *Globe and Mail,* Toronto, Canada: May 19, 1995.

—, "Tougher gun bill expected," *Globe and Mail,* Toronto, Canada: June 26, 1990.

Godbout, Oscar, "62 Ruling Upset Dallas Gun Curb," *New York Times* (1857–current file), November 25, 1963, p. 12.

—, "Wood, Field, and Stream; Sportsmen Fear New Curbs on Guns Following Slaying of President," *New York Times* (1857–current file), November 26, 1963, p. 54.

Goldstein, Kenneth, *Interest Groups, Lobbying and Participation in America.* Cambridge, UK: Cambridge University Press, 1999.

Greenhouse, Linda, "House Passes Bill Easing Controls on Sale of Guns," *New York Times* (1857–current file), New York, NY: April 11, 1986, p. A1.

Grose, Peter, "Rifle Group Head Disputes Need of Gun Controls," *New York Times* (1857–current file), New York, NY: June 8, 1968, p. 16.

Ha, Tu Thanh, "Bitter gun debate silenced as Senate passes control bill," *Globe and Mail,* Toronto, Canada: November 23, 1995.

—, "Firearms registry Ottawa's next project, Bill C-68 passes but Senate plans fight," *Globe and Mail,* Toronto, Canada: June 14, 1995.

—, "Parliament gun bill approved in principle," *Globe and Mail,* Toronto, Canada: April 6, 1995.

Hall, Richard L. and Frank W. Wayman, "Buying Time: Moneyed Interests and the Mobilization of Bias in Congressional Committees," *American Political Science Review* 84: 797–819, September 1990.

Harris Poll, "Do you favor continuing the ban (of assault weapons)?" 2004.

—, "In general, would you say you favor stricter or less strict laws relating to the control of handguns?," 1999–2000.

Hayes, Michael, *The Limits of Policy Change.* Washington, DC: Georgetown University Press. Copyright 2001.

Howard, Ross, "Chretien promises tough gun laws," *Globe and Mail,* Toronto, Canada: May 16, 1994.

—, "MPs vote to tighten gun control regulations," *Globe and Mail,* Toronto, Canada: November 8, 1991.

Howlett, Michael, "Issue-Attention and Punctuated Equilibria Models Reconsidered: An Empirical Examination of the Dynamics of Agenda-Setting in Canada," *Canadian Journal of Political Science* 30(1): 3–29, March, 1997.

—, "Predictable and Unpredictable Policy Windows: Institutional and Exogenous Correlates of Canadian Federal Agenda-Setting," *Canadian Journal of Political Science* 31(3): 495–524, 1998.

Hunter, Marjorie, "President Signs Second Gun Bill," *New York Times* (1857–current file), New York, NY: October 23, 1968, p. 16.

Ipsos-Reid Poll, "Could an event like the Virginia Tech shooting take place in Canada?" 2007.

—, "Should the gun registry in Canada be scrapped, or completely eliminated?" 2002.

—, "Should the gun registry in Canada be scrapped, or completely eliminated?" 2004.

—, "Should the gun registry in Canada be scrapped, or completely eliminated?" 2006.

—, "What were the biggest disappointments with the Liberal governments' accomplishments?" 1995.

—, "What were the biggest disappointments with the Liberal governments' accomplishments?" 1996.

—, "Would you support new gun control legislation proposed by Bill C-68?" 1996.

Jones, Bryan D. and Frank R. Baumgartner, *The Politics of Attention: How Government Prioritizes Problems.* Chicago, IL: University of Chicago Press, 2005.

Kennedy, Mark, "Two-Thirds of Canadians back long gun registry: Poll," *Postmedia News and Global Television.* October 5, 2010.

King, Wayne, "Reagan Favors a Gun Law Rated as Mixed Success," *New York Times* (1857–current file), New York, NY: June 17, 1981, p. A28.

Kingdon, John W., *Agendas, Alternatives, and Public Policies.* Boston: Little, Brown, 1984.

Kopel, David B., *The Samurai, the Mountie, and the Cowboy.* Cerritos, CA: Prometheus Press, 1992.

Krauss, Clifford, "Gun Control Act Wins Final Battle As G.O.P. Retreats," *New York Times* (1857–current file), New York, NY: November 24, 1963, p. A1.

—, "House Approves a Five-Day Wait Before Buyers Can Get Handguns," *New York Times* (1857–current file), New York, NY: November 11, 1993, p. B16.

—, "House Defeats Ban on Weapons," *New York Times* (1857–current file), New York, NY: October 18, 1991, p. A1.

Light, Paul C., *The President's Agenda.* Baltimore: Johns Hopkins University Press, 1982.

Lijphart, Arend, *Patterns of Democracy.* New Haven, CT: Yale University Press. Copyright 1999.

Lindaman, Kara and Donald P. Haider-Markel, "Issue Evolution, Political Parties, and Culture Wars," *Political Research Quarterly* 55(1): 91–110, March 2002.

Lipset, Seymour Martin, *Continental Divide.* London, UK: Routledge. Copyright 1990.

Makin, Kirk, "A gun lobby with no bang, Canada's firearms fans are frustrated by effective opposition," *Globe and Mail,* Toronto, Canada: November 26, 1994.

March, Roman R., *The Myth of Parliament.* Upper Saddle River, NJ: Prentice Hall, 1974.

Matas, Robert and Ross Howard, "Massacre puts focus on gun permits," *Globe and Mail,* Toronto, Canada: September 28, 1996.

Matheson, W. A., *The Prime Minister and the Cabinet.* London, UK: Methuen, 1976.

Mauser, Gary and Michael Margolis, "The Politics of Gun Control: Comparing Canadian and American Patterns," *Environment and Planning C: Government and Policy,* Pion Limited, London, UK, 1992, vol. 10, pp. 189–209.

Mayhew, David R., *Congress, the Electoral Connection.* New Haven: Yale University Press, 1974.

McDonald, Marci, "Anti-gun lobbyists and feminists exploit the Vernon massacre," *MacLean's* (108): January, 1995.

Meier, Barry, "In Renewed Battle Over Weapons Control," *New York Times* (1857–current file), New York, NY: April 26, 1999.

Moon, Peter, "Gun control clamor over legislation called an overreaction," *Globe and Mail,* Toronto, Canada: April 12, 1994.

NBC News/*Wall Street Journal,* "About 10 years ago Congress banned the sale of assault weapons. In your view, should Congress keep or end this ban?" 2003.

New York Times, "A Call Against Arms," *New York Times* (1857–current file), New York, NY: June 11, 1968, p. 46.

—, "New Push for Antigun Law Is Expected," *New York Times* (1857–current file), New York, NY: March 31, 1981, p. A6.

—, "Target: Long Gun Control," *New York Times* (1857–current file), New York, NY: May 15, 1968, p. 46.

Norton, Philip, *The British Polity.* New York, NY: Longman Publishing Group, 1991.

Orth, Franklin L., "Letters to the Times," *New York Times* (1857–current file), December 1963, p. 42.

Pal, Leslie A., "Gun Control," in *The Government Taketh Away.* Edited by Pal, Leslie, and Kent Weaver. Washington, DC: Georgetown University Press, 2003, pp. 233–63.

Pettigrew, Thomas F., "Our Society Is Violent Not By Nature But by Structure," *New York Times* (1857–current file), New York, NY: April 28, 1968, p. SM112.

Pew Research Center Poll, "Would you favor or oppose a law that banned the sale of handguns?" 1993–2008.

Picard, Andre, "Concordia head urges pistol ban," *Globe and Mail,* Toronto, Canada: September 23, 1992.

—, "Concordia rector seeks Tory candidates' views on gun control," *Globe and Mail,* Toronto, Canada: April 28, 1993.

—, "Quebec police asked to deny gun permit Concordia, faculty association wrote letters about accused," *Globe and Mail,* Toronto, Canada: August 27, 1992.

—, "Rock backs chiefs on gun curbs, Justice Minister stops short of pledging to cover all firearms," *Globe and* Mail, Toronto, Canada: August 26, 1994.

Pierson, Paul, "Not Just What, but When: Timing and Sequence in Political Processes," *Studies in American Political Development* 14: 72–92, 2000.

Pralle, Sarah B., "Timing and Sequence in Agenda-Setting and Policy Change a Comparative Study of Lawn Care Pesticide Politics in Canada and the US," in *Comparative Studies of Policy Agendas,* London, UK: Routledge, 2008, pp. 29–47.

Pross, A. Paul, *Group Politics and Public Policy.* Toronto: Oxford University Press, 1986.

Reinhold, Robert, "Effort to Ban Assault Rifles Gains Momentum," *New York Times* (1857–current file), New York, NY: January 28, 1989, p. 1.

Roberts, Steven V., "A Ban on Gun Parts Is Urged in Congress," *New York Times* (1857–current file), New York, NY: April 1, 1981, p. A21.

—, "Kennedy Set to Compromise to Obtain Gun Control Bill," *New York Times* (1857–current file), New York, NY: April 2, 1981, p. A22.

—, "Rifle Group Viewed As Key to Gun Law," *New York Times* (1857–current File), New York, NY: April 5, 1981, p. 31.

Sabatier, Paul A., "Political Science and Public Policy," *PS: Political Science and Politics* 24(2): 144–56, 1991.

Salisbury, Robert H. and Kenneth A. Shepsle, "U.S. Congressman as Enterprise," *Legislative Studies Quarterly* 6(4): 559–76, November 1981.

Schattschneider, E. E., *The Semi-Sovereign People.* Hinsdale, IL: The Dryden Press, 1960.

Schuman, Howard; Stanley Presser, "Attitude Measurement and the Gun Control Paradox," *The Public Opinion Quarterly* 41(4): 427–38, Winter, 1977–78.

Seelye, Katharine, "Bill to Ban Some Assault Guns Seems Headed for House Defeat," *New York Times* (1857–current file), New York, NY: May 4, 1994.

—, "Clinton's New Gun Proposals Include Charging Parents of Children Who Commit Gun Crimes," *New York Times* (1857–current file), New York, NY: April 27, 1999, p. A20.

Sinclair, Barbara, "The Role of Committees in Agenda Setting in the US Congress," *Legislative Studies Quarterly* 11(1): 35–45, 1986.

Soroka, Stuart N., *Agenda-Setting Dynamics in Canada.* Vancouver, BC: UBC Press. Copyright 2002.

Spitzer, Robert, *The Politics of Gun Control.* Washington, DC: CQ Press, 1988.

—, *The Politics of Gun Control.* Washington, DC: CQ Press, 2004.

Stimson, James A.; Michael B. Mackuen; Robert S. Erikson, "Dynamic Representation," *The American Political Science Review* 89(3): 543–65, September 1995.

Stout, David, "Clinton 'Shocked and Saddened,' Hopes for Prevention," *New York Times* (1857–current file), New York, NY: April 21, 1999, p. A.17.

Time Poll, "Overall, do you think that gun control laws in this country should be more strict than they are now, less strict, or are gun control laws about right now?" June 6, 2011.

Tolchin, Martin, "Congressmen Sit in Stunned Silence After Hearing of Attempt on Reagan's Life," *New York Times* (1857–current file), New York, NY: March 31, 1981, p. A4.

Toner, Robin, "Renewed Scrutiny for Gun Controls," *New York Times*, New York, NY: April 17, 2007, p. 25.

Walgrave, Stefaan; Frederic Varone; Patrick Dumont, "Policy with or without Parties? A Comparative Analysis of Policy Priorities and Policy Change in Belgium, 1991 to 2000," *Comparative Studies of Policy Agendas*, London, UK: Routledge, 2008, pp. 63–81.

Wearing, Joseph, "Guns, Gays, and Gadflies: Party Dissent in the House of Commons Under Mulroney and Chretien." Paper presented at the Annual Meeting of the Canadian Political Science Association, University of Ottawa, May 31–June 2, 1998.

Weinraub, Bernard, "Bush Explains His Shift on Gun Control," *New York Times* (1857–current file), New York, NY: March 18, 1989, p. 7.

Wildavsky, Aaron; *Politics of the Budgetary Process.* New York, NY: Little, Brown, 1964.

Wilson, Deborah, "Minister denies plan to dilute firearms bill," *Globe and Mail,* Toronto, Canada: February 9, 1991.

Wilson, Rick and Roberta Herzberg, "Negative Decision Powers and Institutional Equilibrium: Experiments on Blocking Coalitions," *The Western Political Quarterly* 40: 593–609, December 1987.

Wilson-Smith, Anthony, "When Marc Lepine massacred 14 women, he shook a nation and sparked an anti-gun crusade," *MacLean's* (112): December, 1999.

Winsor, Hugh and Tu Thanh Ha, "Chretien speaks out for firearms control, 'I believe we have to force everybody to register their guns,'" *Globe and Mail,* Toronto, Canada: October 22, 1994.

Yates, Jeff; Andrew Whitford, "Institutional Foundations of the President's Issue Agenda," *Political Research Quarterly* 58: 577–85, December 2005.

York, Geoffrey, "Gun bill called step backward," *Globe and Mail,* Toronto, Canada: May 30, 1991.

—, "Gun law called tribute to massacred women, Senate gives speedy approval to bill," *Globe and Mail,* Toronto, Canada: December 6, 1991.

—, "Ottawa to change gun-control bill: Justice Minister says redrafting will permit quicker passage," *Globe and Mail,* Toronto, Canada: March 17, 1991.

—, "Two sides prepare for intense fight over gun bill legislation," *Globe and Mail,* Toronto, Canada: June 1, 1991.

Websites

www.cfc-ccaf.gc.ca
www.enotes.com/gun-violence
www. guncontrol.ca
www.nfa.ca
www.pbs.org
www.parl.gc.ca/LegisInfo/BillDetails
www.PollingReport.com
www.thomas.gov

Abbreviations

Bureau of Alcohol Tobacco and Firearms (BATF)
Member of Parliament (MP)
National Firearms Association (NFA)
National Rifle Association (NRA)

Index

ABC News/*Washington Post* poll 53–5,
    58, 59
agenda setting 6
    in Belgium 25
    in Canada 31–5
    comparison of United States and
        Canada 129–30
    degree of public indifference
        and 24–5
    discretionary windows 33–4
    in egalitarian societies 37
    focusing events, role in *see* focusing
        events, role in agenda setting
    Gallup poll *see* Gallup poll
    garbage can model 22
    inside initiative model 37
    interest group power in *see* interest
        groups
    mobilization 37–8
    moneyed interests 38
    outside initiative model 37
    policy entrepreneurs and 22–3
    punctuated equilibrium theory 24–6
    symbols, role in 26
    in terms of issue attention
        cycle 25, 29
    in United States 22–31
American Revolution 7
Angus-Reid poll 103
Archer, Keith 44–6
Assault Weapons Ban 13–14, 58–9,
    91–3
Associated Press 82, 83, 84, 85, 89, 92

Baumgartner, Frank R. 23–4, 26–7
Bill C-15 15, 18, 113, 124
Bill C-17 16, 113, 114, 117, 119–20

Bill C-21 113
Bill C-24 113, 142
Bill C-39 142–3
Bill C-51 16, 113
Bill C-68 17, 113, 122–4
Bill C-80 16, 113, 114–19
Bill C-83 16, 113
Bill C-150 15, 113
Bill C-301 142–3
Bill of Rights 7
Birkland, Thomas 15, 23, 27–30, 41
Bloc Quebecois 44, 119, 123
Boyd, Gerald M. 90
Brady, James 5, 12, 42, 92
Brady, Sarah 92
Brady Bill 12–14, 91–3
Brady Campaign 5, 8, 41–2, 131
Breitkreuz, Garry 142
Brooks, Jack 92
Brown-John, Lloyd C. 17, 115, 124
Bruni, Frank 95
Bureau of Alcohol, Tobacco, and
    Firearms (BATF) 12
Burnham, David 89
Bush, George H. W. 13, 90

Campbell, Kim 115–17, 119
Campbell, Murray 122
Canada
    Concordia University incident 16,
        119–20, 125
    historical perspective of gun
        control 15–18
    interest groups 42–3
    Vernon Massacre 17, 123, 125, 127
    see also individual entries
Canadian Charter of Rights 8

Canadian Firearms Action
        Council 122
Canadian Firearms Center 17
Canadian Firearms Registry 17
Canadian Parliament 43–6
    Bloc Quebecois 44, 119, 123
    Conservative Party 44, 114–20
    House of Commons 44–5
    Liberal Party 44, 120–4
    New Democratic Party 44
    party discipline 44–5
    prime minister 45–6
    Senate 45
Canadian policy-making process 31–5
Canadians for Gun Control 116
CBC News 142
CBS News/*New York Times* poll 58
centralization of power 2, 25
Chahal, Mark 123
Chretien, Jean 17, 121
civil liberties 7, 8–9
Clark, Attorney General Ramsey 86
Clerous, Richard 114
Cleveland Elementary School
        firing incident *see* Stockton
        Massacre
Clinton, Bill 4, 13–14, 94
Coalition for Gun Control 5, 16, 40,
        42, 116–17, 119, 122–3
    vs NRA 130–2
Cobb, Roger W. 27, 37
Cohen, Michael 22
Columbine High School shooting 14,
        29, 81, 94–5
concentrated power 2, 48
Concordia University massacre 16,
        119–20, 125
Congressional Index 22, 59–60, 136
Conover, David W. 90
coupling 22
Crime Bill 82
Criminal Law Amendment Act 15
Cruikshank, U.S. v. 141
Cukier, Wendy 5, 116–18, 122–3, 142

Dahl, Robert 36, 129
Delacourt, Susan 116, 121

Democrats, the 3–4
    on gun control issue 24
District of Columbia v. Heller 140
Docherty, David C. 32, 122
Dodd, Thomas J. 82–3, 85, 88
Dodd bill 82–3, 85
Dowd, Maureen 91
Downs, Anthony 25, 29, 34
dramaturgical incrementalism 29
Dreyfuss, Robert 94
Dye, Thomas 6–7

Eaton, Leslie 96
Eckholm, Erik 92
Edwards, Chet 91
Elder, Charles D. 27
elective dictatorship 3
Erikson, Robert S. 23

Fabrikant, Valery *see* Concordia
        University massacre
federal regulation 11
Fairbairn, Joyce 118
Finney, John W. 83–6
firearm possession, public opinion on
    in Canada 99–103
    Mauser and Margolis study 104–5
    in United Sates 54–8, 135–6
Firearms Acquisition Certificate
        (FAC) 16
Firearms Act of 1995 17, 122
Firearms Owners Protection Act
        of 1986 12
five-business-day waiting period, for
        handgun purchases 13
focusing events, role in agenda
        setting 26–7, 35, 48, 81–7
    Columbine slayings *see* Columbine
        High School shooting
    criteria for 27–8
    gun bill proposals and 61–5, 79
    gun violence 60–1
    impact on policy change 28
    Kennedy, John F., assassination
        of 11, 62, 81–2, 85
    Kennedy, Robert, assassination
        of 11, 62, 81, 83–5

Killen, Texas Massacre 91–3
King, Martin Luther, Jr.,
    assassination of 11, 62–3, 82–3
and knee-jerk policies 30
and learning by policy
    makers 28–30
9/11 attack and natural
    disasters 30–1
Reagan, Ronald, attempted
    assassination of 12, 42, 81,
    87–9, 92
Stockton Massacre 12–13, 63–4, 81,
    90–1, 93
symbols 26
Virginia Tech Massacre 1, 13–15,
    81, 91, 96, 102
Ford, Gerald R. 84
Fort Hood shooting 136–7, 140
Frankel, Max 85–6
Franklin, Ben A. 82
Fraser, Graham 114–15, 118
Freedom to Serve Without Fear
    Act 139

Gallup poll 31–2, 53–7, 127–8
garbage can model, of agenda
    setting 22, 33
gay rights 116
"Getting tough on guns" 122
Gibbon, Ann 119
Giffords, Gabrielle, attempted
    assassination of 136, 139–40
Glassen, Harold 82, 84
Globe and Mail 51, 115, 119–21, 133
Godbout, Oscar 82
Goldstein, Kenneth 37
Greenhouse, Linda 89
Grose, Peter 84
gun bill proposals
    in Canada
        in 1963–2008 112–14
        Conservatives' approach 44,
            114–20
        Liberals' approach 44, 120–4
        by Clinton 94
    Democrat-controlled Congress
        67–8

between the 88th and 110th
    Congress 62–4
left-of-center parties *see* left-of-
    center parties
Republican-controlled
    Congress 66, 68–70
right-of-center parties *see* right-of-
    center parties
trends 61–5
in United States (1963–2008) 66–70
Gun Control Act of 1968 11, 63,
    86–7, 89
federal regulation and taxation 11
1981 firing incident 12
gun control legislation
    in Canada 5–6, 9, 142–3
    comparison between United States
        and Canada 18–20
    Congressional activity
        towards 59–60
    formulated and implemented gun
        control laws 1963–2008 78
    historical perspective 11–18
    moderate gun control legislation 9
    Reagan's views 89
    Second Amendment of the
        Constitution, United
        States 140–1
    stages of policy process 6–7
    in United States 4–5, 9
gun control proponents 13, 60, 79,
    87–9, 91–2, 120, 131, 141
gun culture, United States vs
    Canada 7–10
Gun Owners Protection Act 1986 89
gun registration 23, 102, 124, 128
Gun Registry 1, 121, 124, 142–3
    support for 101–3

Ha, Tu Thanh 121, 123
Haider-Markel, Donald P. 24
Hall, Richard L. 38
Handgun Control Inc. 5, 87
handguns, owning *see* ownership of
    gun
Harris Poll 57–8
Hasan, Nidal Malik 136

Hayes, Michael 29, 41
Hennard, George J. 13, 91
Herzberg, Roberta 37
high-profile shootings 61
    Columbine High School incident
        see Columbine High School
        shooting
    Concordia University incident 16,
        119–20, 125
    Fort Hood shooting 136–7, 140
    Giffords, Gabrielle, attempted
        assassination of 136, 139–40
    Montreal Massacre *see* Montreal
        Massacre
    Northern Illinois University slaying
        incident 14
    Stockton Massacre 12–13, 63–4, 81,
        90–1, 93
    Vernon Massacre 17, 123, 125, 127
    Virginia Tech Massacre 1, 13–15,
        81, 91, 96, 102
Hinckley, John 12
historical perspective of gun control
    Canada 15–18
    United States 11–15
Hoeppner, Candice 142
House Bill 361 139
House Bill 496 139
House crime bill 84–5
House of Commons 2–3, 44–5, 117, 123
Howard, Ross 118, 121
Howlett, Michael 33–4
Hruska, Roman L. 83
Hunter, Marjorie 86

implementation of policy 6, 34, 80,
    101, 133
inside initiative model, of agenda
    setting 37
Institute for Legislative Action (ILA) 42
interest groups 36–41
    Canadian 39–40
    characteristics of 40
    in firearm debate 41–3
    institutionalized 40
    intense minorities 36
    and mobilization of bias 36–7

moneyed interests 38
NRA *see* National Rifle Association
    (NRA)
    in parliamentary systems 48
    in pluralist systems 48
    pro-change group and/or a pro-
        status quo group 48
    pro-pesticide vs antipesticide
        groups 41
    ruling party as 48–9
    US governmental institutions 46–7
Ipsos-Reid poll 99–103, 127, 143
issue attention cycle 25, 29, 34

Johnson, Lyndon 11, 82–6
Jones, Bryan D. 23–4, 26–7
Just Desserts restaurant shooting 120

Keith-Ross, Jeannie 37
Kennedy, Edward 83, 88
Kennedy, John F., assassination of 11,
    62, 81–2, 85
Kennedy, Mark 143
Kennedy, Robert, assassination of 11,
    62, 81, 83–5
Kenniff, Patrick 119
Killeen, Texas Massacre 13–15, 64, 81,
    89, 91, 93, 96
King,

Martin Luther, Jr., assassination of 11,
    62–3, 82–3
King, Wayne 89
Kingdon, John W. 22, 26
Kleck, Gary 93
knee-jerk policies 30
Kopel, David B. 9
Krauss, Clifford 91–2

LaPierre, Wayne 90, 92
Leahy, Patrick J. 95
left-of-center parties 50, 110–12, 119
    and Coalition for Gun Control 125,
        130
    and Gun Registry 134, 143
    restrictive gun control legislation 4
Leimonis, Georgina 17, 120

lenient bill, defined 60
Lepine, Marc 16
Lewis, Douglas 114
Lijphart, Arend 2–3, 42
Lindaman, Kara 24
Lipset, Seymour Martin 7–8
lobbying effort, of NRA 5, 12, 20, 22,
    38, 39, 80, 82, 85, 92, 95
Lott, Trent 95
Luby's Massacre *see* Killen, Texas
    Massacre
Luo, Michael 96

MacDougall, John 118
MacLellan, Russell 118
Makin, Kirk 122
Mansfield, Mike 85
March, James 22
March, Roman R. 32
Margolis, Michael 9, 104–5, 132
Matheson, W. A. 32
Mauser, Gary 9, 104–5, 132
Mayhew, David R. 23
Mazankowski, Donald 117
McCain, John 136
McClure, James 12, 88
McDonald, Marci 17
McDonald v. Chicago 140
McInnes, Craig 114
McKinley, Everett 85
Meier, Barry 94
Metro Toronto Police Services
    Board 121
Metzenbaum, Howard M. 88
minority groups 3, 10, 36, 42, 129,
    132 *see also* interest groups
mobilization, in agenda setting 37
Montreal Massacre 4–5, 16, 18, 40,
    43, 106
  Conservatives and 114–20
Moon, Peter 121
Moynihan, Daniel Patrick 87
Muchnick, Jeffery Y. 91
Mulroney, Brian 115

National Firearms Association
    (NFA) 6, 10, 40, 43, 115, 117

National Rifle Association (NRA) 4,
    10, 39–40, 87–8, 92
  background 4, 42
  Brady Campaign and 5
  vs Coalition for Gun Control 130–2
  financial position 5
  Institute for Legislative Action
      (ILA) 42
  lobbying effort 5, 12, 20, 22, 38, 39,
      80, 82, 85, 92, 94–6
  membership 5
  political role 4, 94–6
  role in 1994 election 4
NBC News/ *Wall Street Journal* poll 58
New Democratic Party 44
New York Times coverage of gun
    violence 2–83, 85, 88, 133
  Assault Weapons Ban 91–3
  Brady Bill 92–3
  Columbine shooting 94–5
  Gun Control Act of 1968 81–7
  Gun Owners Protection Act 89
  1960s 81–7
  1980s 87–9
  1990s 90–3
  1990s–2008 93–6
  NRA's view 82
  Pettigrew's views 82–3
  Kennedy's views 83
  Virginia Tech Massacre 96
9/11 terrorist attack 30–1
non-firearms owners 105

O'Neil, Thomas P., Jr. 88
Obama, Barack 136
Office of Homeland Security 124
Olsen, Johan 22
Omnibus Crime Bill 1968 86
Orth, Franklin L. 82, 84
outside initiative model, of agenda
    setting 37
ownership of gun 8–9, 12, 137
  Americans, opinion of 58
  ban on 121–2
  Bill C-51 and 16, 113
  Bill C-80 and 16, 113, 114–19
  Republicans supporting 39–40

Second Amendment of the
Constitution and 140–1
semiautomatic weapons and
multiple bullet gun clips 91

Pal, Leslie A. 19, 132–3
parliamentary systems 2–3, 19
Perocchio, John 122
pesticide policy, case study of 41
Pettigrew, Thomas F. 82–3
Pew Research Center Poll 55–6
Picard, Andre 119–21
Pierson, Paul 40
police verification of buyers 13, 15
policy entrepreneurs, and agenda
setting 22–3
policy formulation 6–7, 34, 51
policy legitimation 6–7
policy making
coalition government and 2–3
gun control legislation 4–6
minority groups and 3, 10, 36, 42,
129, 132
see also interest groups
presidential systems vs
parliamentary systems 2–3
pro-change interest group and 1–2
policy windows, in Canada
discretionary windows 33
random windows 33, 34
spillover windows 33–4
political stream 22
PollingReport.com 53, 135
Pralle, Sarah B. 40–1
A Preface to Democratic Theory 36
presidential structure, of the United
States 2–3, 10, 47
presidential systems vs parliamentary
systems 2–3
Presser, Stanley 23–4
Presser v. Illinois 141
Printz v. US 13
Privy Council of Great Britain 8
problem stream 22
pro-change interest group 1–2
Pross, A. Paul 38–9
Protection of Federal Events Act 139

public opinion, on gun registration
control 23–4, 133
ABC News/*Washington Post*
poll 53–5, 58, 59
Angus-Reid poll 103
banning of assault weapons 58–9
Bill C-68, 100–1
CBS News/*New York Times* poll 58
comparison of United States and
Canada 127–9
Gallup poll (1990–2008) 54
Gun Registry 101–3
Harris poll 57–8
Ipsos-Reid poll 99–103, 127, 143
Mauser and Margolis study 104–7
NBC News/ *Wall Street Journal*
poll 58
non-firearms owners 105
Pew Research Center poll 55–6
PollingReport.com survey 53, 135
possession of handguns 54–8,
99–103
right to own a gun 105
punctuated equilibrium theory
24–6, 34
Purdy, Patrick Edward *see* Stockton
Massacre

Question Period in Canada 33

Rathjen, Heidi 119
Reagan, Ronald, attempted assassination
of 12, 42, 81, 87–9, 92
Reid, Harry 96
Reinhold, Robert 90
Republicans 3–4, 39–40
on gun control issue 24
Responsible Firearms Coalition of
Ontario 122
restrictive bills, defined 60
right-of-center parties 50–1, 107–10,
118–19, 134
and Coalition for Gun Control 125,
126, 130
restrictive gun control legislation 4,
114
Roberts, Steven V. 88–9

Rock, Allan 121–2
"Rock's gun control bill facing
    compromises" 123
Roll, John 136
Ross, Marc Howard 37
Royal Canadian Mounted Police 15

Sabatier, Paul A. 27
Salisbury, Robert H. 2
Schattschneider, E. E. 36
Schuman, Howard 23–4
Schumer, Charles E. 92, 94–5
Seelye, Katharine 92, 94
Senate crime control bill 83
Shays, Christopher 95
Shepsle, Kenneth A. 2
Shields, Nelson T. 87
Shields, Pete 5
Sinclair, Barbara 38
Snyder, John M. 87–8, 90
Sobrian, Jules 122
solution stream 22
Sopsich, Ernest 120
Soroka, Stuart N. 31–3
Spitzer, Robert 11, 13, 36, 39
status quo policy entrepreneurs 23
Stockton Massacre 12–13, 63–4, 81,
    90–1, 93
Stout, David 93
symbolic policy 29
symbols 26

taxation 11
Throne Speech 32
Time Poll 135
Tolchin, Martin 87
Tomlinson, David 117
Tydings, Millard 85, 86

United States
  Assault Weapons Ban 13–14, 58–9,
    91–3

Columbine High School shooting
    see Columbine High School
    shooting
Cleveland Elementary School firing
    incident *see* Stockton Massacre
firearm debate, NRA vs Brady
    Campaign 41–2
Firearms Owners Protection Act
    1986 12
governmental institutions 46–7
Gun Control Act of 1968 11–12
interstate sales of rifles and
    shotguns 12
Northern Illinois University slaying
    incident 14
restrictive federal legislations
    14–15
Virginia Tech shooting incident
    see Virginia Tech Massacre
    see also individual entries

Venne, Pierette 116
Vernon Massacre 17, 123, 125, 127
Virginia Tech Massacre 1, 13–15, 81,
    91, 96, 102
Volkmer, Harold L. 12, 91

waiting period, for handgun
    purchases 12–13, 60, 84, 92–3
Walgrave, Stefaan 25
Wayman, Frank W. 38
Wearing, Joseph 116
Weinraub, Bernard 90
Wildavsky, Aaron 32
Wilson, Deborah 116
Wilson, Rick 37
Wilson-Smith, Anthony 16
Winsor, Hugh 121
Wright, Jim 88

Yeo Inquest 16
York, Geoffrey 117–18

CPSIA information can be obtained at www.ICGtesting.com
Printed in the USA
LVOW12*1207261014

410402LV00003BA/12/P